ENCOUNTER WITH

COMPUTING

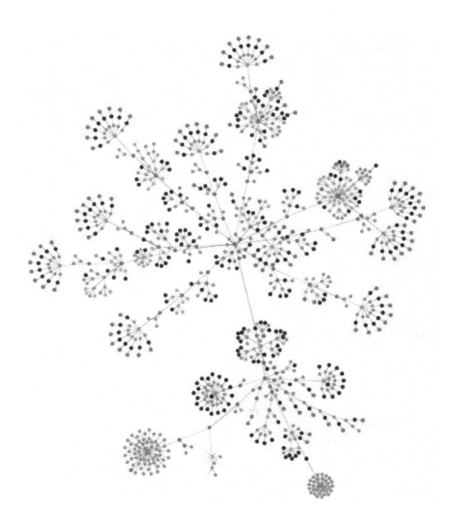

Sarah Harrison and Alan Macfarlane

Contents

Preface to the series

There have been many autobiographical accounts of the creative process. These tend to concentrate on one level, and within that one aspect, the cerebral, intellectual working of a single thinker or artist's mind. Yet if we are really to understand what the conditions are for a really creative and fulfilling life we need to understand the process at five levels.

At the widest, there is the level of civilizations, some of which encourage personal creativity, while others dampen it. Then there are institutions such as a university, which encourage the individual or stifle him or her. Then there are personal networks; all thinkers work with others whether they acknowledge it or not. Then there is the level of the individual, his or her character and mind. Finally there is an element of chance or random variation.

I have long been interested in these inter-acting levels and since 1982 I have been filming people talking about their life and work. In these interviews, characteristically lasting one to two hours, I have paid particular attention to the family life, childhood, education and friendships which influence us. I have let people tell their own stories without a set of explicit questions to answer. This has led them to reflect on what it was in their lives which led them to be able to do their most interesting and rewarding work. They reveal the complex chains which sometimes lead to that moment when they discovered or made something new in the world.

I started for some years mainly in the disciplines I knew, anthropology, history and sociology. But after 2006 I broadened the project out to cover almost all fields of intellectual and artistic work. I have now made over 200 interviews, all of them available on the web. Future volumes based on these interviews are outlined at the end of this volume.

How to view the films

The films are up on the Internet, currently in three places.

Alan Macfarlane's website, www.alanmacfarlane.com

The Streaming Media Service in Cambridge:

http://sms.cam.ac.uk/collection/1092396

On both of these, the full summary of the interviews are available.

Most of the interviews are also up on the 'Ayabaya' channel of Youtube.

The films can be seen from within a free PDF version of this book by pressing on the image. You will need to download an Adobe Acrobat PDF reader (free) from the web if you do not have it. If you right click on the film, other options open up. The free PDF version can be obtained by going to Dspace at Cambridge and typing Macfarlane Encounter followed by the name of the book, for example 'computing' or 'economics'.

Technical information

Unless otherwise specified, all the interviewing and filming was done by Alan Macfarlane, mostly in his rooms in King's College, Cambridge.

The detailed summaries, with time codes to make it easier to find roughly where a passage of special interest is to be found, were made by Sarah Harrison, who also edited and prepared the films for the web.

The cameras improved with time, but there are occasions when both the early cameras and microphones were less than satisfactory. We have had to wait for the technology to catch up.

Introduction

I have had the extraordinary privilege of living through, and actively participating in, one of the greatest knowledge revolutions in history – that of information technology. Being located in Cambridge since 1971, where many important break-throughs have occurred and where such central figures as Charles Babbage, Alan Turing and Maurice Wilkes have been associated with the University, gave me a particular close link to what has transformed our world.

Little did I realize when I first went to enquire in Oxford in 1965 about whether computers could help with the analysis of witchcraft prosecutions in the seventeenth century that huge developments were about to unfold. But when I became a Fellow at King's College in 1971 it was just when an important research project on information retrieval, under the guidance of two Fellows of the College, Ken Moody and Keith van Rijsbergen was under way.

Our historical data formed the basis for ongoing research in the use of computers for social scientists from 1973 for the next thirty years, with several generations of computer scientists working with us to develop database systems. They designed among the first Boolean and Probabalistic (Bayesian) information retrieval systems in Cambridge and later we developed these into multi-media database systems. The story is told in the interviews of Moody, Bacon and van Rijsbergen below.

Meanwhile Cambridge was also more generally the centre of much entrepreneurial work in the making of computers and accessories. This was the time when the science parks began to ring Cambridge. The story of this development is told by two further figures, Andy Hopper and Herman Hauser.

Finally, in parallel, there were developments in improving the computer-user interface. Among those who pioneered in this field was Ben Shneiderman in America, whose interview is included here.

The Cambridge Phenomenon, c. 2010

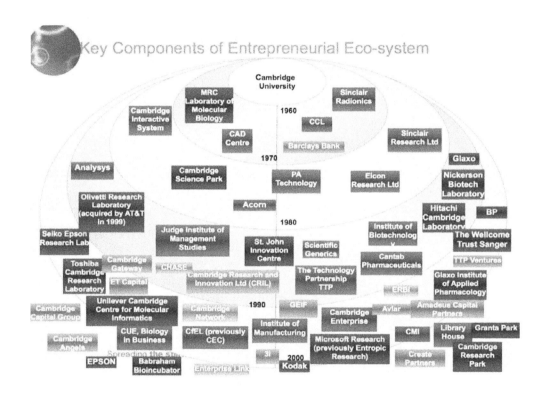

Alan Macfarlane talks about the development of computing in his room in the Old Cavendish Laboratory - 2009

http://downloads.sms.cam.ac.uk/1781750/1781753.mp4

Alan Macfarlane by the Wilkes plaque – Babbage, Wilkes and Computing

http://downloads.sms.cam.ac.uk/1283813/1283818.mp4 -

7

Simon Schaffer on the history and development of computers

Maurice Wilkes on Alan Turing. An after dinner talk at King's College, Cambridge 1st October 1997 (by courtesy of Ian Pratt)

Andy Hopper

22 May 2008

http://downloads.sms.cam.ac.uk/1121912/1121919.mp4

Extracts from Wikipedia – 22.8.2014

Andrew "Andy" Hopper is the Professor of Computer Technology and Head of the University of Cambridge Computer Laboratory.

His PhD was in the field of communications networks and he worked with Maurice Wilkes on the creation of the Cambridge Ring and its successors. Hopper's research interests include Computer Networks, multimedia systems, Virtual Network Computing and sentient computing. His most cited paper describes the indoor location system called the Active Badge. He has contributed to a discussion of the privacy challenges relating to surveillance.

In 1978, Hopper co-founded Orbis Ltd to develop networking technologies. In the same year Hopper worked with Hermann Hauser and Chris Curry, founders of Acorn Computers Ltd; Orbis became a division of Acorn in 1979 and continued to work with the Cambridge Ring. While at Acorn, Hopper helped to design some of the chips for the BBC Micro. When Acorn was acquired by Olivetti in 1985, Hopper became its managing director.

In 1985, after leaving Acorn, Hopper co-founded Qudos, a company producing CAD software and doing chip prototyping. In 1993, Hopper set up Advanced Telecommunication Modules Ltd with Hermann Hauser.

In 1995, Hopper co-founded Telemedia Systems, now called IPV, and was its chairman until 2003. In 1997, Hopper co-founded Adaptive Broadband Ltd (ABL) to further develop the 'Wireless ATM' project started at ORL in the early 90s. In January 2000, Hopper co-founded Cambridge Broadband which was to develop broadband fixed wireless equipment.

In 2002 Hopper was involved in the founding of Ubisense Ltd to further develop the location technologies and sentient computing concepts that grew out of the ORL Active Badge system.

In 2002, Hopper co-founded RealVNC and has served as chairman since the company's inception. In 2002, Hopper co-founded Level 5 Networks. From 2005 until 2009, Hopper was chairman of Adventiq, a joint venture between Adder and RealVNC, developing a VNC-based system-on-a-chip.

Interview Summary

Andy Hopper interviewed by Alan Macfarlane 22nd May 2008

0:09:07 Born in Warsaw, Poland, of Polish parents [1953]; came to the UK in 1964 and was just in the last year of primary school here; my parents divorced and my mother met an English man called Hopper and we came and lived in London; in January 1964 went to primary school in central London; as my mother was working I was looked after by my maternal grandparents [in Warsaw]; they had been middle class before the war but lost everything during the war; my grandfather was an administrative assistant in a church, registering births, deaths and marriages; my grandmother had been part of a family printing business before the war but afterwards was a housewife; went to St Peter's Primary School near Victoria Station; I couldn't speak English and had not taken the 11+ exam; I was rejected by all the private schools like Latymer and Westminster; we moved to Putney and I ended up going to a grammar school in St John's Wood which became comprehensive when I entered sixth form; commuted across London by tube each day on my own; my stepfather, Hopper, is dead; he died almost exactly thirty years ago in 1978; he was a trader in pickled baby beetroot so he had been to Poland on business which was how he met my mother; he also had some retail fruit and vegetable shops and was also a wholesaler of the same in Spitalfields Market; he made a reasonable living and was relatively well off; his first wife died; he was eighteen years older than my mother; when we came to the UK I took his name and an English version of my Polish first name; I retained my fluent Polish because my mother would always talk in Polish when William Hopper, my stepfather, was not in the room; I am very pleased about that and still have an accent which rather suits me; at school, at first did OK then not so well; when I was in lower sixth I was told that I was basically not very able and should do an OND (Ordinary National Diploma); earlier the school had recommended that I went to an applied psychologist who gave me tests which produced that recommendation; they got it wrong as they completely ignored my Polish background; when I had not done so well in my second year, Bill Hopper gave me a financial incentive to do better promising to give me £10 for the first ten places I went up and £2 for each place after that; I came first the following year so collected all he had offered; he was business orientated about education and this may be reflected in my own business interests; managed to get reasonable 'A' levels; not many went to university from this by now comprehensive school; applied to university and ended up at University of Wales, Swansea

10:27:40 Reasonably close to my mother; Polish culture is sticky; don't know about my real father but believe he was some kind of academic; mother fairly ambitious, a woman with attitude, though not particularly pushy; education in that culture is very important, achievement and attainment also important; I always enjoyed the more mechanical, engineering, train sets perspective of things; at school I was kicked out of history very quickly so my knowledge of it is weak; they put me into woodwork; in the late sixties and very early seventies, the first moon landing had happened, and I clearly had some interest in that stuff; you could not get a computer at home at that time and had to go to university to use a computer; I did have electronic kits at home, but in my educational context there was not anything to pull me up; can't remember any teachers who really influenced me; distance of commuting meant that my school friends were narrowed to the area where I lived; I was a cox at rowing; the school was Quintin School, set up by Quintin Hogg who set up the London Polytechnic, and had access to the Polytechnic's sports ground and rowing facilities on the Thames at Mortlake; I am quite sporty and was in the skiing team for both the University of Wales and Cambridge University later on; as I grew up in central London had a good time with friends going to discos; friends were a mixture of Irish, Jewish, some coloured; send my own children to state schools for similar reasons; at a time when computing was starting to get going in a more popular level it did set me up to apply to universities; I applied to Manchester, Lancaster, and Swansea; I didn't get high enough marks for the former but Swansea accepted me; as it turned out that was fantastic because I was good at computing and since then have been top of everything in some broad sense; secondly, David Aspinall, who was from Manchester himself but got his first Chair at Swansea; he set up a course called Computer Technology - I am now Professor of Computer Technology as was Maurice Wilkes - the name is the same but wasn't designed like that; that course was a combination of electronics, computer science and macro-economics; this was 1971 and at an early stage in the subject's development you could for the first time get computers but it was still all to do, to discover, play with - train sets; it was fantastic; Gower, Swansea, wonderful beaches, and socially having been a London person didn't find it difficult to have a good time; during that time I got a car and with a friend drove to Iran and back; he was Iranian and we went to visit his family; the following year went to Brazil by myself and toured; my son is thirteen and just this week is on his first trip to Germany with the school; seems things were easier in my youth; so ended up being on the right course, in the right place; it was rather different to Cambridge as I had never seen a gown until I came here

20:58:19 I did well in Swansea and was still a keen skier, so wondering how I could combine post-graduate studies with skiing; I was planning to go anywhere that was close to a big mountain so didn't apply to Cambridge; I applied to Laussanne and Grenoble but got no response; Professor Aspinall was aware of possible funding difficulties if I applied late in the UK and suggested Cambridge; he knew David Wheeler and suggested I go and see him; came here in early July 1974 when I had an interview with Maurice Wilkes and Roger Needham; the next day they took me; would like to think it was my brilliance but probably they had studentships and somebody had dropped out; this was how I ended up in Cambridge; I duly got offers from places near mountains but I had by then accepted the Cambridge offer; came here in 1974 to start a Ph.D. with Roger Needham as my initial supervisor, but then David Wheeler from the Easter term of 1975; the computer lab. was at a stage where students were not building things which I enjoyed so they set me up with a hardware bench; I had a ski instructor's licence and I went off skiing in December and January; another thing I started doing was gliding; in Autumn 1974 went to the Cambridge University Gliding Club at Duxford and have carried on flying ever since; the Cambridge Ring was one of the projects that I was involved with as a Ph.D. student under David Wheeler and Maurice Wilkes; I was helping with the basic design in the days when there was no local area networks; set out to design one that would connect machines; the Ethernet was just coming along which was a similar idea but done in a different way;

my Ph.D. called 'Local Area Computer Communication Networks' comparing the similarities of networks; came up with the design of a chip which could implement many of these networks using the proposed hardware; this was in 1977 and I was going around explaining how the Cambridge Ring worked as there was a lot of interest in it; set up the link to Social Anthropology to a Nova computer [used by Alan Macfarlane's research project]; at one of the talks met David Thomas of the Rutherford Lab. who suggested developing the chip and offered money to do so; went to see Maurice Wilkes who thought it was a good idea; became a self-funded research assistant to work on the chip; Department of Trade and Industry had an advanced technology scheme which also put money in; as a result, did not finish my Ph.D. in 1977 but in Easter 1978; Hopper died in June 1978 so I didn't actually take my Ph.D. until September; that is how I got into Cambridge as an employee, got into the business of doing chips and networks

32:07:14 Good time to be doing such things in one sense, but the competition was DEC, Intel and Xerox who had got together and 3-Com with Metcalfe in the U.S.; nevertheless, in retrospect as compared to today, where what you do in university as a computer technologist is a little more challenging, it was a good time; it caused a type of technology to exist in Cambridge which later on became a variety of companies, but the roots go back to that; the chain goes as follows: the Computer Lab. is doing the Cambridge Ring, the first time the local area networks are starting; the chip version: find someone to make the chip so use Ferranti who have some hardware but don't know how to design it, which we try to design essentially by hand; we need some computer aided design tools to make these chips; start a CAD project to make the tools to make the chip; meanwhile companies are starting home computing so started CPU Ltd., Acorn was the trading name until it became a public company; CPU uses some of the chips used in the Computer Lab. for the Ring; the BBC Micro having chips inside it is related to that directly; Sinclair used the same chips; BBC micro had a network in it, not the Ring but based on it; Bill Gates came along and we showed it to him and with regard to the network system we were ahead of him; being plugged into the world design clusters, we as Acorn (I was a co-founder with Hermann Hauser and Chris Curry) started doing a microprocessor design which has become ARM, the world's largest supplier of microprocessors to mobiles; for Acorn we needed a CAD so we purchased the CAD project from the University and developed it further into ARM; in the 1900's, another successful Cambridge company called Virata, creating DSL broadband for the home, a networking company that uses a chip for its implementation; all part of a direct line of technologies - Ring -> chip for Ring -> networking -> high tech ventures and businesses

38:38:02 Maurice Wilkes was my Professor and carries on relentlessly with only brief gap in our professional relationship; he was coming up to retirement in 1980 but he still comes in and has an office next to me in the Computer Lab.; when I was running the industrial lab., Olivetti Research Ltd., he had his office next to me there and participated in that; the man is driven; we all have this disease of hunger for success, for impact, a continual desire to achieve something with proper intellectual basis; he is the extreme version - I call him my intellectual dentist because to this day he drills; it is good for me, I know, but it hurts a bit; you can't talk about football with the man; I came in 1974 and he retired in 1980 and he still comes in with technological questions; Roger and Karen Needham - Roger was part of the distributive system on the Ring and was a great systems guy; he was a good leader and had an effect on me; Karen was a little more distant until quite recently before she died as she had been involved with me in fundraising; she also made the first contribution to our fundraising campaign; she was a trustee of various things like the Thriplow Trust with Swinnerton-Dyer and that trust also made a contribution; that was my immediate memory of her but more generally, she helped a great deal with the interdisciplinary nature of the Computer Lab.; I think of her work on language; she and Roger were quite good sparring partners; remember the great party when Roger got his Chair and he went off to do Microsoft; since I used to run an industrial lab. for many years we used to talk about how to run a lab.; the Microsoft situation was different, mine (Olivetti) was a much more independent entity while his was more corporate, yet we could compare ourselves with other distinguished labs. and how we could achieve more than they did; David Wheeler was my supervisor with whom you have a special bond; for the first year I couldn't understand what he was talking about; there was such a gap between what I could offer and where he was, he having done major bits of EDSAC and more; I would pose a question, he would give an answer that I didn't understand so that I had to work out the whole context which gave that answer; in time I could talk his talk; he was very smart and good at detail; he used to scribble on little sheets of paper which we keep in our archives and in my personal archive; it would be difficult in the world today for somebody like that to exist where promotion, recognition and distinction are more formulaic; he became a professor, an FRS and published about three things, but it would be more difficult for him to have become a professor these days; I would have a barbeque at home sometimes and he would turn up on the back of his daughter's motorbike; his daughter wore black leathers which amused us

48:12:09 I started flying in my first year as a Ph.D. student and that takes a lot of time; I like skiing and flying; I have very good spatial awareness and geographical memory, a strong sense of direction and I like tinkering with things mechanical; that matches rather well with flying; the trouble with flying is that it is pretty expensive; fortunately I have made a few bob so I can afford it; I am as professional as I can be about my flying; I've just under 5000 hours flying experience right now which is quite high for someone like me; I fly a single engine Cessna with six seats; I have an airstrip at home, essentially a piece of grass 600 yards long; even though it is a small plane, I can take off and fly to Poland; I don't do aerobatics or racing but I do adventure flying by which I mean travelling; often land in small places where you are as much entertainment for them as they are for you; for example, I have flown all over the Arctic where it is all like that; you can go to some little place in Northern Canada in which case it would be military or a weather station; have been all over South America and Africa, the U.S.A., Canada, Europe, and with luck I'll take it to New Zealand as we are going there for three months next year; for Africa, in say Namibia, you can fly to Skeleton Coast which is 700-800 miles at 50 feet all the way down; I have all the coms so can always phone my mum and check the weather etc.

54:58:14 I have not spent any time at all in India, though I would like to; have been to China on a lecture tour with Gabriel Horn and Tom Blundell; from a business point of view, China's cultural gap is so great that for me, whenever I think I understand what is going on I pinch myself, so I haven't gelled with China in any substantive way; I have been there a number of times with my wife, Alison Smith, who is Professor of Plant Biochemistry; I went to China first in 1977 when it first opened; have been more frequently to Japan; the cultural gap is still large but at least I don't have to pinch myself; at the moment I am developing links with Africa; the good, the arrogant times of technology have moved on; everybody takes the sort of things that I do for granted and assume it will continue; that may not be the case but at the same time more and more people are encompassed by it, have a view and maybe need the technology to develop their standard of living without affecting the planet as their predecessors, us, have done; I am building links for non-charitable reasons, professional business reasons, with Africa; shortly I am off to Cape Town and Kampala where I have personal links; I have had a policy of trying to admit Ph.D. students from the developing world for some time if they are good enough; I have one from Cameroon who has just got a research fellowship at Trinity, Tanzanians, Kenyans; they have to be very good but then they give a perspective on these technologies; for example, we can offer cheap phones to Africans but they want the very latest models and want to be able to afford them; they assume that this will happen and though I think the technology isn't necessarily coming have to give a positive slant to have an impact; it is also an excuse to travel and Africa is great as there is no jet lag

Second Part

0:09:07 The first company I was involved in with Hermann Hauser was the company I sold to Cambridge Ring, one of four companies that were sold to them altogether; that started about the same time as CPU, the company that most people know as Acorn started as well, which was started by Hermann Hauser and Chris Curry; they were in the same place in Market Square as a company called Orbis that I had set up to sell the ring technology, and we amalgamated these companies into one very quickly; I was the smallest shareholder; there I switched to doing work on chips for the computer company rather than working on the ring; Acorn did very well at first then Olivetti came along and took a majority stake; I was one of the directors and they asked me to start an industrial research lab. for them directly rather than work in Acorn; meanwhile I had set up a company called Qudos (quick design on silicone) which had some CAD software for designing chips so was actually a manufacturer of simple chips by using electron beam prototyping onto a surface, each chip one at a time; that joined the living dead though it still exists at the Rutherford Lab.; it could have been a spectacular success but not every one of your companies is so; the thing that we missed was that the hardware side was a very capital intensive business and quite hard and the volumes weren't there as you wrote each chip at a time; the CAD side of the business could have gone global but we didn't prioritise that and now it is a company called Cadence, nothing to do with us; that was about 1985; Olivetti Research Ltd. was set up as a separate company though the budgets came from Olivetti much of the time; I was the C.E.O., the only time I have been; this was all in parallel with my University work first as an assistant lecturer, then lecturer, reader and professor; in terms of my academic colleagues here in Cambridge my career is the most industrial parallel one; when I have started something I have gone with it and done it for a reasonable length of time rather than designing the technology, launching it, and leaving it to others; the research lab. was going very well but Olivetti was not doing so well; we decided we better do something about returns otherwise we would be dead; we started spinning out companies, where you get some research and do it, you assume your team is good enough so you have something that is exemplary; you then offer it to the sponsor, the business unit, and if they don't use it they get a cut, but you try and licence it or open source it to keep it going in some way; technology should not be hoarded; we fell into that cascade of maximizing opportunity by doing all this stuff and at the same time we started getting other sponsors for research in addition to Olivetti; we were not competing with the University; I said to everybody who worked for me (there were about sixty) that if they wanted to be academic they could do the same thing that I did and work simultaneously at both; we didn't pretend to be part of the University but were an applied lab. with more resource; that worked very well; Digital Equipment Corporation and Oracle funded us, we had quite a few suitors and eventually Olivetti sold the company to AT&T and we became the AT&T lab.; Olivetti spawned Virata - Telemedia Systems (which helps with fast editing of multimedia materials), Adaptive Broadband (a wireless company), which spawned Cambridge Broadband (another wireless company of which I was chairman) started in 2000; the industrial lab. was shut by AT&T in 2002; the bad news was that it was completely unnecessary as two people wanted to buy it and it was trashed by its American owner; the good news is that it carries on in several companies, three of which I am chairman, and director of a fourth, because the projects in that industrial lab. were strong and the teams were strong; the people have stuck together, not competing with the University there was a great premium on teamwork in that place; my three companies are RealVNC, a software company, Ubisense, a location technology plus software company, Solarflare, a chip company, and they in turn have spawned Aventiq of which I am chairman, which is another chip company; I am on the advisory board of yet another of these spawned companies; I was directly involved in about a dozen companies in my career and about four at the moment; there is a culture that does go back to Acorn and to the Olivetti Lab. which lasted rather longer than the Acorn culture in its own way; in summary, Acorn did very well and went public; Virata went public and was very successful; some joined the living dead, nothing wrong with that, and some are at the races, and who knows; the ones in play right now are a very motley lot of wonderful companies; what I am talking about is the diversity of each one so for example the 10Gb Ethernet chip company has over $120,000,000 of venture capital; Ubisense has extracted a lot of angel capital and as far as I know is the biggest funded angel company in the UK, £8,000,000; angel capital is personal investment by individuals; RealVNC was originally open source material which now we sell a version of VNC technology for which over 100,000,000 licences have been taken; it was profitable from the beginning and we have kept it small; all this runs in parallel to the University; there is a price to pay on both sides for doing the two; on the University there is not any accommodation for doing the other though I think it is important for the University; on the industrial side you tend not to go with it right to the top level which you could do if you only did that; you are offsetting your risks and enjoying two different worlds; I also do some farming which is quite different; through the University it is non-techie friends who are just as important as the techie friends, but there is a price; you surround yourself with good people and build a level of trust where delegation works; in the University the Computer Lab. takes no time at all compared to running a company; I have just done my fiftieth Ph.D. student and have good post-docs.; it doesn't always gel well in a university system at large, but in Cambridge where you have a strong team group, and on the industrial side I was only C.E.O. of one company, although I did it for sixteen years; you have a broad University radar screen where you can see what is happening in cognate disciplines, your immediate research group which, if healthy, is producing results, the company that is focussed but also part of a multinational side, financing side, knowing how to raise capital

20:49:00 Cambridge is getting less good because of Government pressures, competitive pressures; I am established but a newcomer is confronted with the situation as it is; with my immediate research group it is OK as I can fix consulting etc. for my post-docs. and without that they wouldn't exist in the University; it will be interesting how this develops in the next ten or twenty years; this is compounded by the subject moving on; when I started there weren't hundreds of companies; however, we are still in the University able to do stuff but it takes a little more thought; in the Computer Lab. we have a theme in my own research 'Computing for the future of the planet'; what it asks are what of the engineering or operational approaches to solving some of the major problems, and what role does computing play in it, indeed is computing part of the solution, and indispensable for solving some of these things; imagine observing the real physical world using sensors in great detail and then using that data to optimise some energy cost or something, then feeding that back as a pricing mechanism or just information, that might be an example; if you think of those developing countries, the platform they will have is the mobile phone computer; it may be that by enabling much more wealth creation in that world their standard of living will increase so they won't have so many children; so a method of dealing with population growth among other methods, at least it is one I can do something about; that is a line that is easier to do in the University because even in a large company with loads of money, like Google or Microsoft, even there it would be at the periphery; we have that in the Computer Lab. and I lead the team from behind as it is very important for the Head not to lead from the front

25:01:05 My family: my wife, Alison Smith, her time is just coming with biofuels and how to do it and what does it mean, and GMO organisms and growing things that are appropriate for energy is one of her lines; two children aged thirteen and twelve, a boy and girl; also have a farm with wheat and barley of about 180 acres which I manage

Ken Moody

17 August 2008

http://downloads.sms.cam.ac.uk/1126746/1126753.mp4

Taken from the University website – 22 August 2014

Research interests include distributed database systems, information retrieval, active applications and access control (including RBAC for wide-area applications with federated management domains, and also trust-based access control systems). Jean Bacon and I lead the Opera project, which has had EPSRC funded research grants for the Multi-Service Storage Architecture (MSSA), the IMP Interactive presentation support system, Active Systems, Global Computation using Events, Oasis Access Control, Access Control Policy Management, Business Contract Driven Applications, Securing Publish/Subscribe Information Flows (EDSAC21), Information Management for Patient Care (CareGrid) and the Transport Information Monitoring Environment (TIME-EACM).

Dr Moody has for long been a Fellow of King's College, Cambridge and for many years Director of Studies in Mathematics.

INTERVIEW SUMMARY

Ken Moody interviewed by Alan Macfarlane on 17th August 2008

0:09:07 Born in 1940; mother's family were from Northern Ireland, rumoured to be sheep stealers, and reputedly related to John Adams a participant in the mutiny on the Bounty [who signed onboard Bounty hiding from the law as Alexander Smith]; grandfather was the eldest of twelve children, set for a career in the United Kingdom, but his brothers were sent off to the colonies; grandfather was a customs officer; mother born in Weymouth, then moved to Cardigan where she grew up as a young child; later moved to London and in her teens went to Winchmore Hill Collegiate School for Girls; paternal grandfather, always interested in money, married his first cousin; family originally from the Isle of Wight. My mother was the second of five, the only girl; father was the second of five, the only boy; they married in 1934 and settled in Broxbourne; father worked in his father's business, which was concerned with real estate in Tottenham and was also an accountancy firm; grandfather had done well enough by the mid-1920s to buy a very large country estate in Hertfordshire.

5:22:02 I grew up in Widford, the village of that estate, during the war, so my grandfather was living just down the road, an authority figure; by then my father was dead as he died when I was only a month old; he had a brain hemorrhage at thirty-eight; my mother, who had not worked since their marriage, was a qualified lawyer but was unable to become a solicitor as she could not afford to take the articles; she worked for the solicitors Longmores of Hertford from 1940 until she retired in about 1968 [she actually started working for the Colne Valley Sewerage Board, which was based at Longmores, in 1942; at the end of the war in 1945 she became a full-time employee of Longmores, as a general managing clerk]; the whole of my life was in and around Hertford until I went to Cambridge; mother was clever, interested in literature, a good mathematician; her older brother, Wilfred, was a scientist; he did the statistical estimation for the first traffic lights installed in the United Kingdom at Piccadilly Circus; his son, Frank Adams, was one of the world's great mathematicians; mother was also an amateur actress; later, when in a nursing home, she reacted to the French nursing staff by reciting Baudelaire; she was a terrific person, the centre of my life as I never knew my father; his name was Ken and at birth I was registered as John (after my maternal grandfather) Kenneth (after my father) Montague (after my paternal grandfather); I was renamed Ken after my father died; I had no siblings.

9:54:22 I went to the local kindergarten, Miss Lawson's, in Broxbourne where we were then living [my mother had let the Broxbourne house during the war, and we moved back there in 1945]; there from five until eight; I was taught parsing, tables, a little French, feel that I was privileged; when about three my mother sent me to work out the number of window panes in a window to keep me quiet; I returned alarmingly quickly with the answer, thirty-five, so I must have known either my five or seven times table by that stage; as a mathematician I liked rules so Mrs Pedley, who taught me to parse English, was probably the teacher who was most important in my formative years; at eight I went to prep school, Beaumont House in Heronsgate, between Rickmansworth and Chorley Wood; Peter Vesey, the Headmaster, taught the senior classes mathematics, an enthusiast and a terrific teacher; he was an important person in my life; another charismatic teacher was the Latin master, Vernon Birds, who had fought in the trenches and bore the psychological scars, but had great enthusiasm for the classics; school was quite successful for me, never bullied, and was extremely good at sums; I was also quite good at cricket; Broxbourne had a good tennis club where I played, and later took up squash.

18:16:16 Went to Haileybury [& ISC] in 1953 [on the site of the old East India Company College, with a strong military tradition]; it was between Broxbourne where we lived and Hertford where my mother worked; mother's boss, [Brigadier]

John Longmore, was a governor, and he was able to help with bursaries; without this connection I am sure my mother would not have been able to send me there; in some ways it didn't suit me, but they let me play squash and tennis; Richard Rhodes-James, a housemaster, had been a Chindit in Burma, and was the officer in charge of C company in the Combined Cadet Force; I was a good mathematician in the sense that I could do all the questions; only at S-level did I have any real difficulties; I was lucky that when I entered the A-level course a new mathematics teacher, Stuart Parsonson, was appointed; Frank Newbold who took over as head of maths was a very good teacher but quite traditional; Stuart decided that there were capable people who could do S-level in two years instead of three; I was ready to take the entrance examination for Cambridge at the start of my third year in the sixth; there were a lot of good mathematicians; I was probably the best in my year; Vernon Birds's teaching meant that I came top in Latin in the school at O-level, and feel reasonably confident that I could have done Latin A-level as well as maths and physics, but I was told that if I wished to take Latin I would have to change to classics and learn Greek in a year; so I gave Latin up until I had to polish it up for the Cambridge entrance exam; English changed its nature after O-level, when it became a subject for relaxation in the mathematical sixth form; Jack Thomas would give us interesting books to read and make us talk about them; Bertie Bradstock taught us O-level French and was a real character; I was happy at school.

27:14:03 I was a bird watcher from the age of three; before she was married my mother worked in the Cabinet Office as P.A. to Hubert Henderson, the Chairman of the Keynes group advising on the state of the economy in the depression [(Sir) Hubert Henderson was actually a professional economist who became secretary of the Economic Advisory Council]; Hubert was worried about her brain going to waste after she married, so he got Hope Bagenal, his brother-in-law, a visionary architect, to keep an eye on my mother [Hope was one of the leading acoustical architects of the period; mother prepared the index for his book Practical Acoustics, which appeared early in 1942]; he lived nearby and used to visit during the War, and we would go to watch birds; remember seeing my first kingfisher; I am not a twitcher but always have light-weight binoculars with me, true at both my prep school and Haileybury. At Haileybury on Friday afternoons we were allowed to do things other than games under the heading of public works; I tried building, but later became a printer with E.J. Miller. If you go to a well-organised Colonial Service school thoughts about God are subsumed by the strict timetable for Confirmation; a ritual process in which one moves from being a christened member of the church to being a confirmed member without too much thought going into the process; I went to church with my mother every Sunday; I think she became concerned with the substance as well as the ritual later in life; I could always take or leave the ideas; it was really when I went to university that I started to think about it seriously; one took communion at school, but by the time I left was no longer doing so; I am definitely not an atheist; I get strong theistic moments, for instance, with the sight of ducks on a bright summer's day; I describe myself when pressed as a vague pantheist; I could be a Buddhist more easily than most other religions.

32:09:15 Stuart Parsonson had been supervised by Norman Routledge while at Cambridge, so it was decided that I should apply to King's, where Norman was Director of Studies; I did the entrance exam; did not find all the papers easy but did well enough to get a Major Scholarship to King's; as I still had the rest of a year of school, Stuart Parsonson taught me the first year of the maths Tripos; when I arrived at Cambridge I went straight into prelims to Part 2 so missed Part 1 completely; arrived at King's in 1958; Noel Annan was Provost; for students, he seemed a little pompous and full of himself; the most decisive thing for me going up in October 1958 was the dichotomy between half the entrants who had done National Service and the other half who had not; one moved into an independent, near adult society, which was a social shock; I found going up to Cambridge quite a frightening experience; then I found the ping-pong table, made friends, started playing squash.

39:03:00 Norman Routledge was a charismatic supervisor, a

very capable mathematician, an Assistant Lecturer in the Department of Pure Mathematics; I don't think he got on with his research, certainly he was not confirmed to retiring age and left after a year; I think he was one of the last who lost his chance of an academic career by too much interaction with students; he was one of the founders of the King's loan record library, which was a wonderful resource for students at that period; I learnt to understand and enjoy classical music partly because of the records one could take out for a very small fee, partly because Norman, with Philip Radcliffe, an elderly music Fellow, organised weekly meetings called 'Chats about Recorded Music'; E.M. Forster would participate as well; I remember him listening to Beethoven's Fifth Symphony and recalling what he had written about it in 'Howards End'; good environment as new doors to be opened - too many; there were a limited number of hours in the week and I came to appreciate Dadie Rylands only much later, though lots of my friends did then, as the Marlowe Society were making decisive recordings at the time; on friends - Alan Robiette and I ended up sharing part of a house when we became research students, and we both played cricket; Mike Stevens was another mathematician [of my year] who went off to Canada; he was a dynamic pianist who lived life to the full; I knew John Dunn then although he came a year later; of my year Alan Robiette is the closest; when Routledge was not confirmed, John Williamson moved from Christ's to King's to become Director of Studies; he was a very different character; by then he already had three children and lived in a large house in Hills Road; I got to know the family well; I found his mathematics, which was functional analysis, relatively easy by comparison with that of Philip Hall, who was another Fellow of King's; I attended Philip's Part 3 lectures but did not find them easy; I was obviously cut out to be an analyst rather than an algebraist; Trinity still had Swinnerton-Dyer, and probably half the people that lectured me were at Trinity; my cousin Frank Adams, whom I've mentioned, came back as a Research Fellow there; he later moved to Trinity Hall; I wasn't particularly influenced by Trinity, there were a lot of lectures, but supervisions were arranged within the College and there was a lot of work to do for these; there were mathematics societies and I would go to talks in the evenings if I was interested in the subject, but there was no sense in which I was attached to a particular college group.

46:33:02 I had started at Part 2 so only had to do three years of the four year [Mathematical Tripos] course; I was accepted to do the Diploma in Computer Science in the year 1961-2 but did well enough in my finals [Part 3] to be selected to do research in mathematics; I then did a Ph.D. after which I went off to work for IBM; Margaret Grimshaw was my Ph.D. supervisor, a Fellow of Newnham, and an exceptionally nice lady, but she did very little to drive my mathematical research; I looked to John Williamson who was working in this general area; he had too many Ph.D. students so although I had a problem, I attacked it rather fitfully; I also did a lot of undergraduate supervision, up to fifteen hours a week at one time; it was actually rather irresponsible; John needed supervisors and I did it rather well; he took the view, quite rightly, that I was either supervising or playing squash, and a mixture was better than squash alone; I was all right for money as grants in those days were good; my grandfather had died and left me a legacy though it did not come for some years

51:06:04 I needed a change of career as at that stage, although I had finished my Ph.D., I had not published anything; also I did not have any academic drive, and did not think there was a future for me in mathematics. I went to the Defence Operational Analysis Establishment who play war games; I also met Dr Hugh ApSimon, who had an algebra Ph.D. from Oxford and was a senior academic computer scientist at IBM Hursley; both of these environments offered interesting grounded problems that I was convinced would engage my brain in a way that research in mathematics had never done; King's came to the rescue and made the decision for me; at a dinner I sat next to Philip Noel-Baker, who asked what would be the productive element if I worked for the DOAE, and whether I would be happy with that thought; so I went to IBM; I joined IBM in February 1967 when there were high expectations about the amount of time their staff would put in; they were a paternalistic employer, and having looked at my background decided that I should be recruited to IBM

Government Branch, which ran large scientific machines where my background would enable me to talk to customers; they sent me to the Rutherford Laboratory on the Chilton-Harwell site where I made lots of good friends; there is a story that IBM employees at that period had to wear white shirts and suits; not quite true, as the manager always warned us of a visit a day in advance so that one could dress correctly; I was there for nearly two years, though moved to [AERE] Harwell about half way through; by the middle of 1968 was working long hours, doing very interesting work; the more I learnt about computing the more I realized you only saw the IBM pitch; sometimes you knew that you would have taken other design decisions; having met Hugh ApSimon I was aware that there was a subject, computer science, evolving beyond my horizon, which was a bit unsatisfactory; at the time I had an Australian girlfriend, Anne Howie, and she was still completing a Ph.D. in zoology in Cambridge, so I did go back to Cambridge from time to time; I kept contact with the Computer Lab so knew there was another side to computing that I had no exposure to or experience of.

56:16:20 In 1961 when I had thought of doing the Diploma, Alan Turing was not talked about in King's; probably among the Fellowship, people like A.E. Ingham, a senior King's mathematician, would have remembered him; I think it was a hard subject to discuss because of his ending; there was also Maurice Wilkes in Cambridge at that time, and the Cambridge initiative to build computers was very much in competition with Manchester where Turing had been; Turing was also at the National Physical Laboratory, and these were the three locations in the UK principally connected with the emergence of computing; I did not come across Wilkes as an undergraduate or in 1961 when I went to find out about the Diploma; Eric Mutch, who was then the Deputy Director of the Mathematical Laboratory, was responsible for organising admission to the Diploma, and I spoke with him; I did not know of Wilkes's existence until 1968 when I was at Harwell; I think John Williamson had been talking with Roger Needham, Wilkes's deputy at that stage, about me as someone who might be better suited to an academic career in computing; John Williamson then told me that there was the possibility of a job

in the Computer Lab; he had just got a Chair at York so suggested I could Direct Studies in maths at King's too; another disastrous career move, but I was attracted to both, and it seemed a reasonable combination; however the Mathematical Laboratory said I would need references; did not want to ask any of my senior advisors at IBM as my career there was going quite well; the customer came to mind and I picked the one I knew best, for whom I had done some useful work; I knew nothing about his background - this was John Burren the physicist at Rutherford, and it seemed to me that a half smile crossed his face when I asked him; what he didn't tell me was that he had shared a flat with Roger Needham as a graduate student in Cambridge; not only did he write me a good reference but it hit the right spot; IBM were sorry to see me go and gave me three years of academic absence on the correct assumption that it would not have been a final career decision; I was employed by King's without a Fellowship as Director of Studies, but lived in College.
Second Part

0:09:07 I did not have a Fellowship at King's when I returned but was offered Direction of Studies, and also had a job at the Computer Laboratory as Senior Assistant in Research; paid at the same level as an assistant lecturer with no guarantee of tenure or commitment on either side, but a chance to work in a fascinating environment; the lab knew they were going to have to buy a new mainframe computer; they built Titan themselves, a prototype Atlas 2 machine, but technology was moving so fast and there was no way they could keep up using home built machines; naturally at that time they would be looking at IBM kit, so in some sense I was the purchaser of the future; I lived in King's, in free accommodation, in the Keynes Building [only just completed]; my friend Alan Robiette was then a teaching Fellow in Corpus Christi as was another old friend from King's, Haroon Ahmed; they suggested that as Corpus was short of mathematicians I should take a Fellowship there; King's heard the rumour and made me a Fellow in 1969; by then Edmund Leach was Provost; I soon found myself on College committees, including the Council, and made very good friends there.

4:50:24 I got to know Oliver Zangwill quite well as he lived on the same staircase; I had hitch-hiked at least 100,000 miles by the time I first had a car just before I went to IBM and I would therefore pick up hitch-hikers; after a squash match, coming back from Hertfordshire, I saw a slightly disheveled figure in the headlights; I picked up young Barry whom it became clear was on the run from an approved school, Kneesworth House; I took him to Cambridge and asked where he was going to stay; he did not want to go to the police station, which fuelled my suspicions; I let him sleep in my sitting room; next morning I contacted Gill Macfarlane who told me to take him back to Kneesworth House, which I did; about a year later Zangwill knocked on my door as Barry was again on the run and in his rooms; we decided to route him back through friends he had made while on the run; Zangwill had found him waiting outside my rooms and had entertained him until I returned [Oliver was Professor of Experimental Psychology, so an expert witness to Barry's state of mind - "rather disturbed"]. Experience of Edmund Leach on the Council; his antagonism towards Bob Young; Adrian Wood's warning of a Leach outburst.

14:15:21 When I joined the Computer Lab in 1968 I was working with one particular computing language called Snobol4, which was based on a different model of computation from the classic lambda calculus model; for text processing applications this gave completely different dimensions from a language like Fortran, which was good at doing sums but no good for character strings and character manipulation; there had been a number of earlier languages - Snobol1 to 3 - based on Markov algorithms; by Snobol4 it was a hotchpotch of all known ideas in computing, so had functional programming embedded in it; it had been developed by a group including Ralph Grisbold, who had moved from Bell Labs to the University of Arizona at Tucson; he provided a portable implementation in the form of a macro-processed specification; it was a lot of work to implement it, and this was the first job I did in the Computer Lab; I liked Snobol4; we provided an implementation for Titan and it worked well, and was soon installed on the Atlas2 at the CAD centre; as a technical trick the thing that I am proudest of in all my computing career was porting the Snobol implementation from the Atlas2 back to the Atlas1 at Chilton, where I had worked when I was with IBM; we ported it in binary; the operating systems of the two machines were quite different, so I took the specification of the Atlas1 operating system, generated a version symbolically on the Atlas2, then dropped it into memory with a large patch area where we could fix bugs; there were only three bugs; I worked with Eric Thomas, who had done the Cambridge Diploma before going off to work at the Chilton Atlas, and was very well disposed to Cambridge; we had finished by lunchtime; Snobol gave great service there, because at Cambridge we had plenty of other language support, but Chilton had nothing for text manipulation, so [Snobol4] was very widely used there.

19:37:01 Snobol had no relationship to BCPL, which was a minimalist language in the lambda calculus tradition; I shared an office with Martin Richards who developed it; BCPL was the language that led to B at Bell Labs, which was followed rapidly by C [; when the Lab purchased an IBM mainframe in the early 70s I was the natural person to help Martin port BCPL to the IBM 370 architecture]. I first thought that what [Alan Macfarlane was] doing with historical data was inherently interesting when I saw your card index in King's in 1973; you showed a set of cards relating to a particular village family; I was surprised that from early demographic records one could get such a dense coverage of family relationships and lives; I was interested as I like practical problems; thought it would be a little-computer-project, also I had begun to get interested in database management systems; the language side was interesting because the languages we were working with at that time did not have good support for text processing, or like Snobol, were a bit of a mess; two things to be addressed - managing this very large set of data and finding languages that would support social scientists; I really enjoyed the problem, and in terms of career development I was very lucky to have access to an excellent undergraduate, Tim King, who just as we were beginning to formulate the project was finishing his degree; we had interest from IBM who had a prototype relational DBMS called PRTV

[Peterlee relational test vehicle], which was under development at the IBM Scientific Centre at Peterlee; we set up a joint project; no one had experience of using relational databases for such a complex set of character string data - about 13,000,000 English words - an awful lot of date for the time; also it was from a wide variety of parish sources, and the problem of telling the story and extracting information without damaging the nature of the data is something that really intrigued me; I remember insisting that whatever was done we should retain access to the original text of the records; it would have been possible to encapsulate snippets onto punch cards, but that would not lead to the greatest benefit; right from the start we aimed to put the records in, abstract the natural language meaning by marking the records to say what was meant but retaining the word structure; with the benefit of hindsight that was obviously right, but at the time it looked slightly ambitious given the size of the data.

28:05:19 Charles Jardine [a former King's Maths student] who worked on the mark-up and query languages was clever, zany, highly innovative; as far as I can tell totally unambitious, but intrigued by problem solving; I always found him a delight to work with because he repeatedly made you laugh; Tim was not laid back but brought enormous abilities; he had sufficient competence and confidence as a programmer to say that PRTV was not working as it ideally might; we had an architectural model derived from PRTV that we really liked, namely the use of relational algebra as the basic language representation; PRTV was one of a number of prototype relational database management systems in the mid-1970's. The relational model had been spun off from a paper, an intellectual idea developed by Ted Codd in 1970; the amount of software required to drive the model is vast; by the mid-1970's there was a system called Ingres at Berkeley, developed by Michael Stonebraker, also an IBM project System R being developed at the San Jose Lab, as well as PRTV; both Ingres and System R were developing around a language called SQL, which was related to the relational calculus, essentially a record by record model for analysing relational data; PRTV had gone instead to a relational algebra model that allows you to write queries in terms of whole relations, that is all of the records satisfying particular constraints or in a particular format; for technical reasons, if you have got a large number of updates and you are going to have to manage concurrency control, a relational calculus approach is preferable; the great beauty of our problem in its matching with PRTV is that we were interested in setting up a database that was the model of the records describing Earls Colne, then exploring the database to derive the model of what Earls Colne might have been like; the great beauty of this is that there is no update, fundamentally a read-only database; for our purposes a relational algebra model was far more suitable. The way in which they had set up the implementation of relational algebra was to use recursive calls down a tree representing the parsing of a relational expression; for various reasons this is not nice, because it interferes with natural concurrency flow during evaluation; Tim had the idea that we should retain relational algebra, exploit the parse tree in a rather similar way, but instead of doing recursive calls from the top of the tree we should set up an active co-routine structure and allow the data to flow as it naturally wished to; that is what we did; it meant reengineering the whole of PRTV, which we duly did in BCPL; Martin Richards and I devised the co-routine structure and wrote a paper in 'Software Practice and Experience'; we have a research student currently working on similar problems and he has developed extensions to Java; out of curiosity I showed him this 1979 paper and the resonance with what he is doing now is surprisingly close; I think the computer science that came out of the project was real and good; quite recently I went to Cardiff for the 25th anniversary of the British National Conference on Databases; I found that there on the list of the issues that would be discussed in the review of twenty-five years of British computing was CODD, the Co-routine Driven Database that Tim developed, and CHIPS, the Cambridge Historical Information Processing System that was the rather over-elaborate high level language that we designed to support queries to this database; so we certainly made a mark on the community; there was a later paper describing the database implementation on top of the co-routine support; it taught me a lot about things like how you get grants; it made me publish something at last; it was excellent experience in terms of introducing database technology into the Lab; the fact that there was national level profile for the work pushed the Lab towards database, which previously they had no experience of; once again I go back to the fact that the work is driven by the data - the inherent interest in that made us all excited; Jessica King and Sarah Harrison's work on the data quality and preparation sides.

40:32:11 Later on [1998] came Tim Mills, who wanted to do a Ph.D. in information retrieval, a phenomenal developer of code; he wanted to take existing retrieval engines and generalize them, retaining the architecture of the engine, the matching functions, the evaluation, and the use of feedback support, but applying them to collections of data that were other than text documents, e.g. images, photos, which might contain annotations as well; I was interested in that aspect although I had not kept up with the basic literature on information retrieval; Keith van Rijsbergen had worked with me as a Ph.D. student much earlier, had gone to Glasgow and had become a leader in the mathematical end of information retrieval and the processing that went along with it; I knew what Keith was up to and had enough programming sense to know that Tim Mills and I would get on fine; that was the case, and he submitted two months short of his three years as a Ph.D. student; as one of the things that he did, he needed a test data set to study, so we took the original Earls Colne data and provided an IR context within a Web site; that was not the original purpose of Tim's Ph.D. but it was proof by example that what he had done worked. Keith van Rijsbergen did work on probabilistic retrieval when he came back to the Computer Laboratory as a Royal Society Research Fellow; it helped to make his reputation; Martin Porter, who was a former Ph.D. student with Karen Spärck Jones, worked as a Research Assistant on Keith's Royal Society project; I wasn't close enough to their work to comment in detail; I met Martin professionally later in the mid-1980's; my former girlfriend, Anne Howie, was associated with setting up a Chinese-English paleontological thesaurus [actually the baby of a colleague of Anne's at Monash University outside Melbourne, Pat Rich]; I got involved because the Cambridge end, which was responsible for dealing with the printing of the English side, was supported by the Literary and Linguistic Computing Centre; for various reasons things were not going well, and Martin Porter came and helped me then; we ended up publishing it; both Charles Jardine and Martin Porter are very clever, but neither is at all ambitious.

49:10:00 In the 1970's the Cambridge Ring was just happening; we had a relational database engine that operated by taking a parse tree and deploying the individual nodes to locations that were supported by co-routine activations and communicated with one another; this allowed the natural data flow to control the concurrency, rather than having it imposed by recursive call from the top of the parse tree; Tim had the very smart idea that since we had this architecture, there was no reason why the node representations should even be in the same processor; if you had something like the Cambridge Ring you could do your parse, generate a parse tree and then activate the nodes at different machines in the processor bank, allowing them to communicate through the Ring; in the same way as when I got Snobol to work straight away, we deployed it on the Ring and it evaluated quite a complex relational expression without any trouble; it was a validation both of the Cambridge Ring and of the co-routine structure that we had been using; IBM's original model would not have had a cat in hell's chance of making sense of what was going on because it was too complicated; one of the other things that was happening was that the Cambridge Distributed System was being developed in the 1970's; this was the software exploitation of the Cambridge Ring communication technology and the processor bank computational model that went along with it; lots of people had one, it wasn't just us, but everyone who had one suddenly found that they could do interesting and original things. The screen editing system goes back to the efforts that we made to mark the natural language structure of the records and the entities in the records that carried meaning at application level; there was a particular group within the Computer Laboratory, led by Charles Lang, which had a lot of experience with the PDP11 system, and we developed an interactive text editor, first on the PDP7 then on the PDP11, for extending the text documents with diacritical marks; I think other people were doing this but arguably we were among the first - some of that work certainly anticipated SGML and therefore XML, so I could say it is all our fault.

53:53:00 I took one consulting job only; I have always valued my time and have always had enough money to live on; the exception was when I bought a new house in 1977, a three-hundred year old thatched cottage in Knapwell, west of Cambridge, which needed a lot of work done on it; the consulting job was implementing BCPL on a Siemens processor, which was quite like an IBM machine but with a completely different operating system, in the EU in Luxemburg; in three weeks I earned a third of my annual salary and paid for all the building work. My wife Jean's contribution to my career has been enormous; she came to the Lab in 1985; she had worked very much in these areas of concurrency and distribution; she did a Ph.D. as a member of staff at Hatfield Polytechnic; she knew all about the theory and the practice, and she programmed and made things happen in the world that took off in the 1970's; by the 1980's she had made her reputation in that area; embarrassingly enough I was on the Lab interviewing panel that appointed her, though I did not know her before that; early on we started working together as we have similar areas of interest; I discovered to my shock that she would almost always rather write a paper than write code; I had regarded the paper as something one wrote when one had run out of ideas; the result of meeting Jean was that we started writing papers together; we had research students that had begun to form a group; Jean encouraged them to write and their reputation spread; we were quite early into distributed event-based systems, also federated application management and the access control structures that are needed to support it; these ideas have become more and more important; all of these things are driven by technology revolution to some extent; in the 1980's we were developing distributed database management systems, absolutely miserable quite early into distributed event-based systems, also federated application management and the access control structures that are needed to support it; these ideas have become more and more important; all of these things are driven by technology revolution to some extent; in the 1980's we were developing distributed database management systems, absolutely miserable to work with because moving data from one place to another was a total labour; all of this was made redundant by the comms revolution; suddenly there was no trouble in getting data moving from A to B; there are still concurrency and consistency issues, but you were not bothered by the slowness of the technology; we were exploiting the new model early and it has stood us in good stead, and we have run a happy group since 1988. Jean had never liked my thatched cottage, and in 2003 we moved to Blythburgh as our second home; the option of autonomy was no longer there, so we got married.

Herman Hauser

3rd September 2008

http://downloads.sms.cam.ac.uk/1120413/1120420.mp4

Extracted from Wikipedia – 22 August 2014

Herman Hauser is probably most well known for his part in setting up Acorn Computers with Chris Curry in 1978. When Olivetti took control of Acorn Computers in 1985[13] he became vice-president for research at Olivetti where he was in charge of laboratories in the U.S. and Europe. In 1986, Hauser co-founded the Olivetti Research Laboratory (ORL) in Cambridge along with Andy Hopper who became the laboratory's Director. In 1988, Hauser left Olivetti to start the Active Book Company.

In 1990, Hauser was involved in spinning out Advanced RISC Machines (ARM) from Acorn. In 1993, Hauser set up Advanced Telecommunication Modules Ltd with Andy Hopper. The company was acquired by Conexant Systems on 1 March 2004. He founded NetChannel Ltd in June 1996 as a holding company in order to begin work on marketing the NetStation. NetChannel was sold to AOL in 1996. He claimed in the 1990s that the networking technology used for AppleTalk was based on the (unpatented) Cambridge Ring.

In 1997 he co-founded Amadeus Capital Partners Ltd, a venture capital company, and in 1998 he co-founded Cambridge Network with David Cleevely and Alec Broers. In 2000, Plastic Logic was founded, with Hauser as chairman.

In August 2004, Amadeus Capital Partners led the Series B venture capital financing of Solexa, Ltd and Hermann Hauser joined its Board of Directors. Solexa developed a next-generation DNA sequencing technology which became the market leader. Solexa was sold to Illumina, Inc (ILMN) of San Diego in January 2007 for over $600M. In 2009, Dr. Hauser was announced as the first customer of the Illumina Personal Genome Sequencing service. As of 2009, Dr. Hauser is the head of the East Anglia Stem Cell research network.

Dr Hauser is a Non-Executive Director of Cambridge Display Technology Ltd, a Non-Executive Director of XMOS Ltd and a Member of the Board of Red-M (Communications) Ltd. He is a member of the Advisory Board on the Higher Education Innovation Fund, and of the UK's Council for Science and Technology.

INTERVIEW SUMMARY

Hermann Hauser interviewed by Alan Macfarlane 3rd September 2008

0:09:07 Born in Vienna in 1948; great-grandfather born in Brno, Czechia, apparently walked from there to Vienna with all his possessions on his back; on his grave stone described as house proprietor and burgher of Vienna which were obviously the two things he was most proud of; this, my mother's side, has been Viennese ever since; my father's family is Tyrolean and for many generations have been farmers and innkeepers; during the War my mother's family decamped to the Tyrol because Vienna was being bombed and occupied by the Russians; she stayed at a farm near my father's home and that is how they met; I was the first son; I grew up in the Tyrol in a place called Wurgl near Kufstein; its claim to fame is as a railway junction from Germany to Innsbruck and from Innsbruck to Vienna; grew up in a tiny village, part of Wurgl, with two to three hundred inhabitants; my parents had a very strong influence on me; my mother moved back to Vienna after my father's death as she loves the city; my father was in many ways the exact opposite; he was a country boy and an entrepreneur; he built up a wine wholesale business; I suppose a lot of my own entrepreneurial urges come from the fact that he talked about the business issues; he gave us the feeling that the buck stopped with him and that he was ultimately responsible for the business; in my own life I have been pretty successful but even so there is a large amount of risk, and on average about 30% of companies never make it and people lose their jobs; fortunately we now have a wonderful environment in Cambridge that Andy Richards described as a low risk environment to do high risk things in; if people fail in a Cambridge company, because there are so many high tech companies the chance of them getting another job is quite high

6:18:22 My parents were originally religious in the way that all Austrians were and it was part of our social fabric that we go to church on Sundays; later, as was the case in my school, the Gymnasium in Kufstein, there was a dramatic change in ordinary Austrians' attitude to religion which also affected the way my parents lived their religious life; during the eight year period that I was at the Gymnasium there was a change from the dominant position of the Catholic church, where the most important person in the school was the priest, not the Head, but who was an irrelevance by the end of that period; people did not become anti-religious but it just disappeared from their live; we stopped going to church but no one really talked about this change; I recently read both Dawkins 'The God Delusion' and 'The Dawkins Delusion?' which was interesting because it reminded me of my own thoughts in regard to religion; on one hand I found the former quite liberating to say one is an atheist, which I suppose I am, on the other hand I felt he was overdoing it by suggesting one had to fight religion which I could not identify with; I suppose I became a little disillusioned with religion in Austria as it had become social habit rather than something that was thought through; I remember meeting Steve Furber, one of the brightest people who ever worked for me, one of the inventors of the ARM, now Professor at Manchester; he is religious, he is clearly a lot smarter than I am, so if somebody as smart as him believe then it must be valuable to him and I have to respect that

12:10:20 My first school was the primary school in Bruckhusl, a wonderful village school; we had up to three years in one class; my mother forgot to tell them that she wanted me to go to the Gymnasium which was academically a highbrow thing to do; when she finally told them they were all excited as they hadn't prepared me for the entrance exam; I got private tuition and just made it into the Gymnasium; primary school is from six to ten and Gymnasium from eleven to eighteen; Frau Edelstrasser was a wonderful first teacher; she was beautiful, kind and knowledgeable; I can remember her sitting beside me showing me how to form letters; I developed a love for physics because of my uncle who had studied both physics and maths at university; there few jobs for mathematicians after the War so he became the local jeweller and watch repairer in Wurgl; when we went on mountain walks together he would tell me about physics and maths, that you could turn lead into gold but that no sane person would do it as you needed an atomic reaction; he talked about atomic physics in particular and the discoveries of quantum mechanics; at about fifteen-sixteen I bought myself a book by Zimmer about quantum physics and relativity which we were not taught at school; I was good at both physics and maths; I always participated in games, particularly faustball (fistball) which we played in the courtyard of the Gymnasium; I took up squash here but learnt tennis in Austria; I have skied since I was four; I run once or twice a week around Granchester; music is important; we had a wonderful music teacher called Kurt Neuhauser who was quite a famous organist who was widely broadcast on Austrian radio; he was totally absorbed in music who became exasperated if his pupil could not understand him; Mozart was taught, so was Haydn; I developed a taste for Bruckner and Mahler, then Stravinsky; having lived here for a while, discovered Vaughan Williams; Chris Curry with whom I started Acorn Computers is very patriotic and said that Vaughan Williams did not write music for foreigners; people point out that he is in business with a foreigner but he describes me as an honorary Brit

22:57:21 We have our thirtieth anniversary of Acorn Computers on 13th September, and while looking for some pictures, I discovered that I must have come here first in 1964 when I was only fifteen; I came to the Studio School in Cambridge on a language course; my father had come back from Innsbruck thinking that I should learn English as it was the most important language in the world; now I tell my children to learn Chinese which they are doing; I first did my military service which was still compulsory in Austria and did my first physics degree at Vienna University; important person for me there was a man called Roman Sexl, a gravitational expert who also wrote text books for Austrian schools; I specialized in gravitational theory for my first degree; Walter Thirring had just returned from CERN as the head of theoretical physics there; his lectures were wonderful for their clarity; one was on electromagnetism where he generalized Maxwell's equation in a concise manner; during the summers, because I had been to Studio School I returned to Cambridge because it had impressed me so much at fifteen; looking back I just can't believe that my parents put me on a train at Wurgl to go to Ostend, by ferry to Dover and train to London, then another to Cambridge; I arrived and had found my lodgings then two days later wrote a postcard to my parents to tell them; this would reach them a week later; when my kids arrive in Beijing and don't phone immediately I get very worried; apart from one summer in Paris, learning French, I came back to England every summer, always to Studio School; after the third year I asked John Morgan, a teacher there, what I should do and he suggested taking a Russian course at the Sidgwick site, which I did

28:52:20 During my time at Vienna I became a research assistant during the summer at the Cavendish Laboratory; a wonderful experience as they treated me very well and I could do some interesting experiments; since the results were encouraging, when I finished at Vienna, they suggested that I do a Ph.D. here; I was with John Field's group in physics and chemistry of solids, in David Tabor's department; we were near the Hopkinson Lecture Theatre in the Old Cavendish (where social anthropology is now); my father had been keen for me to do economics and take over his business but he was always very kind and realized I wanted to do physics; he was not an academic and didn't know how to make the decision for me; he went to see an acquaintance, Klaus Draxler, who was an assistant lecturer in physics at Vienna University; Draxler said that my school results were good enough to do physics but warned me I would never be rich, and that I would be much better off doing economics and going into my father's business; at eighteen I accepted that I would never have any money but I would do physics

32:31:04 My Ph.D. was on laser induced reactions; we would fire a laser at a surface and see how plasma would form and whether or not this could trigger an explosion; we were using high speed cameras which were taking picture at the rate of 1,000,000 per second which at that time was by far the most advanced high speed photography possible; I went from quite a theoretical background in gravitational theory, via my research assistant work to something that was applied; I ended up by applying a new computer analysis method for thermal balance and differential scanning calorimetric data that I got for chemical reactions; there is a thing called the 'Hauser Method' which is a lazy way of getting all three reaction parameters out of a single experiment; my supervisor was John Field who was very helpful, particularly when writing up the thesis, but he was a practical rather than theoretical person; David Tabor was a great linguist and would always stop on the way to his office and speak to me in German; Brian Pippard's lectures were clarity itself, but the person I probably learnt more physics from was a Ph.D. student who finished a few years before me, Jacob Israelachvili, who became a professor at Santa Barbara; he was the first person to measure van der Waal's forces right down to microscopic distances; these are forces that are very important, particularly in biology

36:45:22 Andy Hopper was doing computer science at about that time; we had met socially and played tennis together; I did the Fortran courses that many physicists did at that time, I used the IBM 360 mainframe and before that the old Phoenix system; even used the Titan system before the IBM came with a teletype interface which we had in the lab; I think I was one of the first people in Cambridge to bind in computer output directly into my thesis as part of the trick of doing the three reaction parameters in one experiment was to do a graphic output and use the graph to find the reaction order; knew Maurice Wilkes well; had the pleasure of offering him a position at the Olivetti Research Lab when I had become Vice President of Research at Olivetti after Acorn Computers; Maurice had returned from DEC after five years and was interested in a position in Olivetti which Andy Hopper headed up; he has been seminal for Cambridge computing; he was one of the first computer scientists in the world; his work on microcodes in particular forms the basis for all the microprocessors that Intel produces right now; it wasn't until the early 1980's that there was a new and different approach to microprocessors, used by ARM, the RISC approach - reduced instruction set computer; until then all microprocessors used microcoding which was his invention; he started the first Diploma in Computing; at that time the computer laboratory was called the maths lab; it changed its name to computer lab under Roger Needham; I had great respect for Needham and really appreciated the way he interacted with local businesses; at that time we had just started Acorn Computers at 4A Market Hill, about 200 yards from the Computer Lab; one of the best investments I ever made there was Fitzbillies' buns in the afternoon for anybody who wanted to come, which meant that half the computer lab was at Acorn at four o'clock in the afternoon; they normally stayed and one of the traditions at that time was that whenever I got hungry they would

get a meal off me if they were still there; a lot of the breakthroughs
- and there were lots of them, Acorn was a very innovative
company - were made in the Italian Kitchen a few doors down; one
of them was the Econet - one evening we invented networking;
thought that computers should talk to each other and got terribly
excited in linking them all up in a local area network and we
designed it; then Andy Hopper walked in and we showed him the
design on a serviette; he looked at it and said it would never work
and redesigned it; it was this change that led to the most successful
area network in Britain at the time; we had 10,000 installed
Econets in British schools in 1980-1981

43:12:42 Although Acorn doesn't exist any more, one of the
reasons for the Cambridge phenomenon is the Acorn philosophy;
we were really a systems company; we designed our own chips,
hardware, computer, operating system, application software; we
were the only computer company at the time to have a local area
network; Bill Gates saw it and our BBC computer and he wanted
to sell us MS Dos; told him that it would be a retrograde step as
our operating system was way ahead at the time; one could get files
off a server that was far away using the same method as to get files
on and off a floppy disc; Bill's response to that was "What's a
network?"; manipulating images came later; people often forget that
in those days the BBC computer came in two varieties, Model A
and Model B; A had 16kb of RAM and B had 32kb; now just the
caches of microprocessors are typically 1mb; we had word
processors running; lots of books in Cambridge were written on
BBC micros; we had spreadsheets, graphics - typically line graphics
- but there was no way you could do video or high resolution
pictures; Ethernet is a local area network, invented by Bob
Metcalfe, typically 100 metres of cable; internet is global; World
Wide Web invented by Berners-Lee while working at CERN in
order to share results between researchers all over the world; in a
way we are witnessing a repeat performance with the Large Hadron
Collider where the amount of data is so vast that they have built a
much higher speed network called the Grid to get the data out to
lots of research groups all over the world

48:19:24 After my Ph.D. I had two serious options, one was to apply for lectureships in physics, the other was to go back into my father's business; although I had done physics he had never given up the hope that I would finally return; my younger brother later did take over the family firm after graduating in economics; at that time I met Chris Curry socially; he was working for Clive Sinclair at the time and was getting a bit fed up; Clive invented the business model, among other things, that Chris introduced at Acorn, to sell computers through mail order; that was how we could finance Acorn without venture capital or any large sum from the founders; Acorn was an unusual company in many dimensions; one of them was that the total amount of investment that it had was £200, £100 from Chris and £100 from me; therefore it is the only company that I know of that had a capital gain of a million-fold; when we went public at £200,000,000 every pound we had put in was worth £1,000,000; Andy came in later; he and I had a company called Orbis Computers which we merged with Acorn which is how he became the third director; after my Ph.D. I had a research fellowship at the Cavendish for a year; I must have absorbed some of my father's business skills because it felt very natural when we set up Acorn Computers; I did not feel apprehensive about starting a company; we started the Cambridge Processor Unit (CPU) first in 1977, and a year later, Acorn Computers; to begin with we were living hand to mouth; CPU was a consultancy and our business plan was that it was all happening in microprocessors; we were very excited by the possibilities as were the Cambridge microprocessor group where we hired the best and brightest; the true skill which I brought was my ability to find out who the really bright people were that could produce a really good computer and then convince them that they should join Acorn Computers; the excitement at that time was similar to the excitement about the internet twenty years later; I recognised the same sort of people, same attitude to life, and belief that it was going to change the world; we knew that microprocessors would change the world and the idea of bringing microprocessors to the people, of letting them have access to a personal computer - at that time called a home computer and our customers called enthuserasts; our first product had a key feature, that it must not work; if the kit they received did not work, then the customer would have the satisfaction of making it work

56:37:20 Acorn was the first company in Britain to go from zero to £100,000,000 in revenue in just five years so it was a phenomenal success; everybody thought we were walking on water, articles suggested we had the Midas touch, and if this goes on you start to believe it; none of it was true it was just that the market was exploding at that time; then came 1984, the year that the home computer market collapsed, just at the time we had solved the only problem Acorn Computers had in its whole five year history, which was to produce enough; we finally had them coming in by the lorry load but they were not going out any more; we got into very serious financial trouble and Olivetti finally took us over; Acorn was restructured and they offered me to become their vice president of research, which I did; I moved to Italy, to Ivrea, and had the first boss I have ever had in my life Elserino Piol, the vice chairman of Olivetti, which was a wonderful experience; he taught me about venture capital, business, a great strategic thinker; he was the person who turned Olivetti from a seven billion dollar computer company to a zero billion dollar company at the same time that he created Omnitel and made it leap from a zero billion dollar mobile phone company to a twenty billion dollar company; it was the most dramatic change in a corporate strategy of any Italian company; he also had a corporate venture arm which invested in American companies, and I would always travel with him and we would do these deals together, so it was an apprenticeship for becoming a venture capitalist; he was also a very clear thinker, almost at a strategic level; we communicated in English although it took time to realize that he was speaking English

Second Part

0:09:07 Problems associated with information retrieval; first came across the problem when a student in Vienna; read book by Rudolf Carnap, 'The Logical Construction of the World' and what impressed me was that he started with a single concept of the recollection of similarities through which one could build up all the other concepts that we have in our language, basically by set theory; we now know that Bayesian probabilities is probably a much more elegant way of approaching it; one of the things that I would like to do sometime in the future is to see if we could build a computer that is a probabilistic computer rather than a traditional microprocessor; I hope to put together a group of people to help me think about it including Steve Furber and Steve Young who has been working on speech recognition and that is all probabilistic in Markov chains; we have a wealth of people who know about Bayesian arithmetic; a most valuable company in Cambridge now, Autonomy, run by Mike Lynch is based on Bayesian principles, and we have a very strong group in the Engineering Lab on that; I really think it such a fundamental problem, possibly the most fundamental problem of intelligence that I would like to do more work on it

3:35:02 At Olivetti, I had seven research laboratories all over the world; before taking the job I had spoken to Philip Hughes who ran Logica at the time, who advised me to take it and to learn how big companies worked; it was the right advice; those three and a half years were some of the best in my life; they treated me very well and I had great freedom to do what I wanted; I set up the Olivetti Research Lab here with Andy Hopper; I had another in Palo Alto and in many other places, but the one in Cambridge was by far the most successful; Alfred Marshall the teacher of Maynard Keynes did an interesting study on clusters in Manchester around the textile industry; he famously said that this knowledge about how to do textiles was in the air because people would be constantly talking about it; in Cambridge we have had a few seminal companies like Cambridge Instruments, Sinclair Radionics; Acorn, and CCL, that became the companies that set the gene pool; the Judge Institute did some very nice work on the relationship of the companies that have been formed over the last twenty years and the original company that they worked for; Acorn alumni are responsible for over a hundred companies in the Cambridge area; Acorn plays a similar role in Cambridge to Fairchild's role in Silicon Valley where all the big semi-conductor companies in the Valley are "Fair children"; the overlap between the University and commercial companies is one of the things that really distinguishes Cambridge from other European universities, and sadly, because of the obsession with conflicts of interest, in the United States, too; Roger Needham was a classic example of somebody who from personal experience was unbelievably helpful to Acorn Computers in the early days; he allowed us to employ people in the Computer Lab on a consultancy basis; some of the chips in the BBC Micro were developed in the Computer Lab by people who were lecturers and they were consulting for us; he also allowed his students to be fed Fitzbillies' buns and spend a bit of time with us; he would come to me for little bits of financial help in the Lab which we gave him; it was totally informal but both the Computer Lab and Acorn benefited from it; at that time it was informal as people trusted each other; it has become a bit more formalized but it needed to as the stakes are higher and the companies bigger and the contracts need to be more precise, but there is still a willingness on both sides to be supportive of each other; sadly, especially many continental universities, don't do that, and have an aversion to work with business

11:39:00 A few years ago there was a great debate about intellectual property rights; the most important thing was that the University decided on clear rules on how to do this; one of the problems we had before was that you couldn't actually go to the University and ask to pay for intellectual property rights and base a company on it because they would not know who the IPR belonged to; they could neither give a licence for it as they couldn't say they owned it, nor say that they didn't own it so go and do it; all they could say is that they didn't know; that particular problem was solved so there are now clear rules; this clear rule set is now being implemented by a subsidiary of the University called Cambridge Enterprises; think we have been quite lucky in the person who heads it, Teri Willey, because she had done a similar job for Chicago University and has spun out a group into a venture capital firm that did that for Chicago, and she has a non-confrontational personality which suits Cambridge; my hope is that this will lead to more spin outs, but there are more rules and it is more regimented than in the past; the IPR arrangements in Cambridge are the most generous in Europe, and more so than both Imperial College, London, and Oxford, and I think that is a good thing; there is movement between Berkeley, Stanford and Silicon Valley, but their IPR arrangements are much tighter than here; however, there are one or two universities in America allow IPR to be used freely rather than assuming that it belongs to the university; cannot see much difference in spin outs between this type and the rest, so both work;

16:10:16 On spin out companies, I did not set out to have so many links but they just happened over the years; I suppose it is partly because of Acorn Computers and partly because during the 1980's and 1990's when there wasn't a lot of venture capital around I suppose I was about 50% of the angel money; they knew I was a sucker for technology and if they came to me with an interesting project I would try my best to either fund it myself or find them funding; I am always happy to speak with people even if I don't find funds for them as I am always interested in new projects and new technology; set up a venture capital fund, Amadeus, in 1997, at a time that people did not believe in technology venture capital, especially not in Europe; all the money we got came from America although now most comes from Europe; people then did not believe there was enough deal flow but I knew there was as I had too many projects to cope with; Richard Friend and Plastic Logic; raised the largest amount ever, $200,000,000, for the company which I set up with Richard Friend; we had built the world's first plastic electronics factory in Dresden, Germany, which will be opened on 17th September; it is quite an historic event because it will be the first time in fifty years that a new semi-conductor goes into mass production; the last semi-conductor was silicon and here is a new one made out of plastic; it came out of work in the Cavendish Laboratory where Richard did his Ph.D. just one year after me; we have a new product called an e-reader that I think will change the way that people read; it is a product category between a personal computer and the mobile phone; it is clearly lighter and you can hold it in one hand easily; you will be able to change pages by touch and it is very paper-like; it is a reflective rather than emissive display like a lap top, and because it is reflective display and bistable, it consumes no power at all when you read it but only when you change the page; means that this unit will probably have an endurance of three weeks; there will be two models, one 2gb the other 8gb; the latter will hold 2,000,000 pages, so about 10,000 books; it has three main uses, e-books, e-newspapers and the paperless printer; people are emotional about books and accuse us of trying to destroy them; I am reading a book on molecular cell biology at the moment in bed, but there are 1000 pages so it is the most awkward thing to read, and weighs 5kg; it would be much better if it were 300g, and easy to hold in one hand; it has many things in common with paper; one is that it is reflective and therefore you can read it under any lighting conditions; in particular it is very good in sunlight where personal computers are no good; secondly, the contrast ratio between black and white is 10:1, exactly the same contrast ratio to paper and because it is bistable it does not flicker at all, so people have a reading experience which is as close to paper as any display that has ever been invented; we have over seventy-two patents; it has a Bluetooth and Wi-Fi interface as well as a USB so when you connect it to your computer you will have a shared folder so anything in it will be synced to the e-reader; there is a search function on the e-reader itself and you bring up a keyboard by touch interface and type in the search query; you can type in data but this is not the aim; the Kindle is a 6" display whereas this is 11"; the former weighs the same although a lot smaller; this is lighter as it is the first implementation of plastic transistors whereas the others have glass as a substrate where we have polyethylene; if you tried to produce a display of this size in glass it would be very much heavier and would break easily

27:09:18 Richard Friend's group in the Cavendish Lab have been unbelievably productive; they first invented polymer organic light emitting diodes which went into a company called CDT (Cambridge Display Technology) which I was also involved in which was bought by Sumitomo; the second spinout was Plastic Logic with Henning Sirringhaus, one of Richard's brilliant students who is now a professor himself at the Cavendish; Richard has a wonderful new approach to photo-voltaic cells, again based on plastics rather than silicon; I am very excited about that, and maybe we can produce another company; the energy problem is so big and this is such a neat, long-term solution; all the others, perhaps with the exception of wind, are band-aids; using the sun which had been the provider of energy on earth for the past four and a half billion years, it is a wise thing to use; the main advantage over solar panels, which use silicon, is cost; silicon is about 20% efficient now and plastic solar cells are about 6-7% efficient at present, so we need to get their efficiency up; people like Richard have a wealth of experience in the electronic structure of polymers so I have every confidence that they will be able to increase the efficiency rapidly over the next few years

30:20:13 There were six founders of the Cambridge Network which straddles the business community and the University; the University was one of the founders and it was set up with an objective of bridging the gap between academia and the business community; it now has over a thousand companies as members, all the Departments of the University are members; there are open lectures for both academics and business people as contributors; it has a vibrant web site and newsletter; we didn't expect it to be so successful when we founded it some ten years ago with the help of Alec Broers; it is also concerned with how Cambridge presents itself to the rest of the world so has a close relationship with the Munich Network, Shanghai Network, Stanford Network and one or two others, so is part of a network of networks; it runs the corporate gateway so connects well to big companies; Kodak came here because of it, so did Nokia; an unexpected boon is that the web site has now become the main jobs web site for companies

32:55:00 The early attraction of Cambridge was the girls and punting; I was at King's for my Ph.D.; one of the really nice things about Cambridge was that, as an Austrian with a bit of an accent, you were accepted here - not odd, but interesting; when people ask me which organization I identify with in Cambridge, it is really King's because I lived here, had lots of student friends here, and the exposure during formative years creates the bond; I am proud of the University, the Cavendish, but the strongest emotional bond is with the College; Herbert Huppert, as another physicist, I have stayed close to; I had a nice relationship with Alan Bilsborough who was my tutor at the time; at one point I thought I wanted to change from physics to artificial intelligence; he gave me a lot of good advice and introduced people for me to talk to; a lot of artificial intelligence work was being done in the King's Research Centre and he introduced me to people there; in the end I thought it better to finish the Ph.D. and then do something in computing, which I did; Pamela, my wife, like Alan Bilsborough was a physical (now called biological) anthropologist; first met her in the King's bar and we married in the Chapel

36:35:24 Over the past twenty years the high tech environment in Cambridge has blossomed; people often ask me what I thought about the next five to ten years; I am quite optimistic about it; think that many of the building blocks that made Silicon Valley so successful are finally in place in Cambridge; there has never been a problem with technology but there was a real problem with management, we just didn't have experienced managers; we now have many second generation serial entrepreneurs; an interesting data set is that in Amadeus I 17% of the deals that we did were with serial entrepreneurs, in Amadeus II this had risen to 40%, and now in Amadeus III it has risen to 70%, all in just ten years; so we have home grown talent we can now work with and we can also attract some of the best managers from all over the world; so Solexa, our latest billion dollar company was grown by a John West who ran a billion dollar operation of ABI, the lead company in sequencing machines; we went to him as a little Cambridge start-up saying we had a machine that was a hundred times better than the one he was selling, and that we wanted him to sell ours; he looked at the machine, and as a physicist understood the technology, and agreed; for Plastic Logic I just hired the most senior person I have ever hired in my life, Rich Archuleta, who ran a ten billion dollar business for HP; this was something that we couldn't do ten years ago; we also have technology based venture capital, like Amadeus, to put syndicates together; there is also a local culture now of people who are quite willing to engage in start-ups - a low-risk environment to do high-risk things - so people can dare to join a start-up which might have a shaky future as if things don't work out there are enough other start-ups where they can get a job without having to move; the other criticism that people make is that there are not any more interesting things to do; I have never seen more exciting new projects as I am seeing now

40:19:22 The belief that China will build what we dream up is a very short-lived phenomenon; they clearly don't just do Nike shoes; one early example of that is a company they called Huawei which produces telecoms equipment and is now one of the largest in the world; a few years ago they had a huge court case that Cisco brought against them because they were copying Cisco kit, Cisco being the largest provider of network equipment in the world; now

Cisco hopes to copy what Huawei is doing because it's kit is now ahead of Cisco; they are the innovators now, Cisco the follower

Jean Bacon

16 September 2008

http://downloads.sms.cam.ac.uk/1109583/1109590.mp4

From Cambridge University website – 22 August 2014

I'm Professor Emerita of Distributed Systems at the University of Cambridge Computer Laboratory. I lectured systems courses such as "Concurrent Systems", "Operating Systems", "Distributed Systems" and "Computer Architecture". Author of "Concurrent Systems" Addison Wesley, 1st edition 1993, 2nd edition 1998, which in 2002/3 evolved into edition 3 for the Open University's "Software systems and their development (M301)" and "Operating Systems: Concurrent and distributed software design" with Tim Harris.

I'm a Fellow of Jesus College and Director of Studies in Computer Science.

I'm a Fellow of the IEEE and a Fellow of the British Computer Society. I was elected to the IEEE Computer Society's Board of Governors for 2002-2004 and 2005-2007. I was founding Editor in Chief of IEEE Distributed Systems Online (DS Online), which was extended from 2008 to become Computing.

My research interests are in the broad area of distributed systems. Ken Moody and I led the Opera research group from its creation in the 1990s.

INTERVIEW SUMMARY

Jean Bacon interviewed by Alan Macfarlane 16th September 2008

0:09:07 Born in Stocksbridge in the Pennines in 1942; lived in a village outside the town up a hill until I was six, so started hill walking as soon as I was able to walk; still take walking holidays in mountains, looking for flowers; grandparents died before I was born or when I was very young; working class background, one grandfather a stone quarryman and the other a steel worker; father worked in the steel works all his working life; he was very quiet and self-contained; he didn't drink having witnessed the effects on his father; a Methodist; mother also very quiet; tragic that she was never able to work; she is now ninety-one and is very bright and could have done so much given the chance; she loved school but both parents had left school at fourteen; they did Gilbert and Sullivan operas with a local group and there were chapel events; I am the only child; my mother was quiet possibly because of my father; since his death she has done much more socially in the chapel

4:14:07 First school was Green Moor Primary School where there were two classes, infant and junior; I left before the junior class; remember the teacher, Miss Henson; think she was a supply teacher and she was very kind; remember being far more advanced in mathematics when I went to the big school in Stocksbridge, so must have been taught something; I think I liked sums as I was always asking for them before I was six; also liked drawing and picking flowers, and combination has been part of my life ever since; at Stocksbridge I took the 11+ a year early, and went to Penistone Grammar School at age ten; they had an accelerated programme so that the A stream got to the sixth form a year earlier than the rest so I was there at fourteen; had taken 'O' levels before that; I always put maths as my top subject but also spent time in the art room; there was also an excellent sixth form library which I used to educate myself; nowadays I would be the sort of person who did double maths, English and art, but at that time you had to do arts or sciences, so I did double maths and physics; there were good teachers - Mr Stone who did physics, Mr Whitehouse then Mr Senior who did maths; there was a stern headmaster when I first went there, Mr Bowman, and his wife did the maths classes for the scholarship pupils; it was a mixed grammar school; we still have reunions and my particular year meets every couple of years even now; there are some academics amongst us and lots of interesting people; I think Oxbridge scholarships were always thought a possibility, other than university it was teacher training college; I didn't try for Oxbridge but got a scholarship to Royal Holloway, London University and went there in 1960 at the age of 17 after three years in the sixth form

8:37:12 At school I hated sport and have never been terribly musical although I enjoy listening to it; Mozart, Beethoven and Schubert are among my favourites; music has never affected my mathematics; think I am an English and art person rather than a scientist deep down; do think that the way music communicates emotion is strange and is similar to the way in which colours convey mood - all in the same domain; when at school was counter-suggestible so did question faith; for a long time it made me anti-dogma and anti-church; I did not have my son baptized as I did not think it should be imposed on him; I regret this now as he wishes that I had just done it so that he did not have to decide; I don't go to church regularly but like going into churches because I love old buildings; had an exhibition in Blythborough Church and sat there for a fortnight, and loved it; I am not an atheist but cannot believe in the religious significance placed on the human race; what I take from religion is the inter-personal relations; not really sympathetic with Dawkins' view about proof

14:27:10 Went to Royal Holloway to study mathematics; with hindsight I should have gone to a mixed college in the centre of London; having been at a robust, mixed, northern grammar school, a women's college twenty miles from London diminished my enjoyment; the work was alright; I painted a lot ñ the grounds were beautiful; I had come across computing and computers through vacation jobs and it was mentioned at school, but there was no opportunity for any statistics or computing in the course; it was very much classical mathematics; I did not want to stay on and do an MSc or PhD at that stage; I did vacation jobs between 1960-63 at United Steels in Sheffield, Stafford Beer was doing work study there and they were very much into cybernetics; they may have used the University computer or were about to get one, but they sent me on a course at Sheffield University for a couple of days; found it very easy to do assembly level programming; found it intriguing and encouraged me to go to the National Physical Laboratory for my first job

17:17:19 At Royal Holloway there were some very good lecturers; Professor McCrae was a relativity specialist, and I did that option, but there was nothing that made me want to carry on with it; I then went to the National Physical Laboratory at Teddington; I was in Mathematics Division and came across the people who had worked with Alan Turing after the war; people like Jim Wilkinson were still there, and they had worked with Turing on the design of the Pilot ACE; when I was there, the manufactured version, the ACE, was what was being used and the English Electric DEUCE, so companies had started building computers; the ACE was in a huge room with huge numbers of racks of delay lines; the Pilot ACE is now in the Science Museum, but the ACE that people were using to do numerical analysis and machine translation, you booked time on it and sat at the console, looked at the green lights and tried to debug your program, a very primitive way of operating; input was probably by paper tape but I went on a course to learn to use both tape and cards; the programming language was Assembler; it was horrific as the instructions were going round a delay line and took a different amount of time depending on whether they were additions or multiplications, and you had to put the next instruction just after this instruction finished; at that time had no idea where all this was going but did become evident that computers would be used for other than scientific purposes; during wartime, the Colossus computer was used for code breaking; interestingly, Alan Turing couldn't admit that he knew about that as it was still secret, so when he went to build the Pilot ACE after the war they believed it would be difficult to engineer and that nobody knew how to do it; the people who had been at Bletchley Park did know but they couldn't say; they did it but it was difficult to convince people without revealing what they knew; think that Turing is a colossal figure in computing because of his contribution to the theoretical side but also to the engineering and design side as well; he was reputedly a difficult person and left NPL and went to Manchester; the Turing test is to tell whether a computer or a person is interacting in a blind interrogation; Chris Evans at the NPL later did work on medical diagnosis by computer to see whether it was possible to automate the process; my job there was writing programs for numerical analysis; the computer memory at that time was tiny; the ACE had 7000 vacuum tubes; the technology had to go through core store subsequent to delay lines, then transistors; think it is when chip development started and transistors were used was when Moore's Law kicked in; transistors came in about fifty years ago; the IEEE Computer Society timeline of computing goes back to pre-War computers and shows when all innovations, such as transistors, were first used; EDSAC was developed by Maurice Wilkes; the way I saw it from the NPL, there were three British computing projects in progress; there was the Pilot ACE, ACE and DEUCE at NPL; there was then Turing's next attempt at Manchester 'Baby', and EDSAC at Cambridge; these three were all operating in the late 1940's; it was an exciting thing to be working on and all three projects were contributing; there was a lot going on in America at the same time at about the same level

27:12:04 Stayed at NPL for only a little over a year; I met my first husband, Mike Bacon, and married in 1964; we had the two job problem; he moved to Dollis Hill where he was working in the Bletchley Park subject area; I had to find a job and went to GEC Hirst Research Centre so that we could live and work in that area; I was doing aerial design so got a job as a mathematician; I was working on frequency modulation and such things; where I got back into computing at GEC was using the London University Atlas between 1964 and 1968, another very interesting computer; at that time there were very few machines which was why I was using it; I enjoyed using the Atlas and later went on to teach about its architecture and met some of the people who had designed it, including David Howarth and Frank Sumner; by 1968 was thinking about the two body plus child problem, so went into lecturing, firstly at Watford Technical College; at that time we used the Elliott 803 machine at Hatfield Polytechnic; I did a masters in computer science at Hatfield part-time and then got a job there; Hatfield was early into computing and had a big national presence in it; I was teaching machine architecture, using a lot of Assembler; Hatfield was just about to get the DEC System-10 timesharing system so I taught that; part of my masters at Hatfield was about the DEC10 machine code and when I went to lecture there I was teaching the architecture and programming at that level; by then it was obvious that computers were developing very fast but were still mainframe; one was having to acquire new skills all the time; it is difficult to remember before you had a computer on your desk, how you got computer time, how you queued up for it; suddenly things got so much easier; Hatfield was a very good place to be with many good people; those that taught me became colleagues; Roger Sharp was Head of Department and Gordon Bull, very dynamic and forward looking, John Lewis, very competent and aware of academic politics, all very good people; it was not a huge department though there was a lot of pressure to expand after I left in 1985

33:48:02 I was never part of the drinking culture that was evident among computer scientists although I encourage my students to talk together and discuss work; I tend to work very hard then relax by painting; at Hatfield we had the mainframe then were early into buying minis; the first one was built in Stevenage; then we went on to the Motorola 68000 as a teaching machine, so had many of them in the labs; the potential for them being joined up prompted my PhD; in the 1970's we started having local area networks (which Andy Hopper talked about); going back - at the NPL in the mid 1960's they invented packet switching - Donald Davies - and interacted with people in the States who were building the Arpanet which became the Internet, so the NPL has been a very influential place over the years

36:54:23 I got my PhD in 1981 and I got interested in connecting computers together; I was just using serial lines as simple connections but was aware of the developments in Cambridge with the Cambridge Ring, and in the States with Ethernet; instead of the packet switching wide area networks that were slow and unreliable at that time there was a move towards local area networks; Cambridge was very much connected with work in America; Roger Needham went to Xerox PARC (Palo Alto Research Center), later DEC, regularly over the summer and had great friends there working in computing where they exchanged ideas; Xerox PARC was well ahead with Ethernet-based systems; they put a work station on everyone's desk although no one could afford it at that time, just to see what would happen; this spawned the Alto computer, then the Dandelion and the Daybreak, but there were problems as they did not exploit them commercially; Apple very much arose out of Xerox PARC research; PARC were starting to develop good human interfaces (GUIs) - the mouse, icons - so the research background was evolving at Xerox PARC; [Steve Jobs did not work at PARC. After visiting there he was convinced that GUIs were the way forward and went on to create the Lisa.]; my PhD was on distributed systems, so looking at the operating system kernel and how you include communication, and how you had processes running on distributed components interacting with each other; so looking at the potential of not only one program on one machine, but where you had more than one machine how you got the components to interact; my supervisor was Adrian Stokes who had a PhD in computer science and was teaching at Hatfield at the time; he now works in the National Health Service; I got a part-time PhD in three years; a lot of the work was project supervision as well so I could get code written by project students; I moved up from lecturer, to senior lecturer to principal lecturer at Hatfield; it seems a huge teaching load when you consider lecturing separated from supervision at Cambridge; I had a teaching load of 15 hours a week which included splitting the group you lectured to into several tutorials, having them do case studies on operating systems; I did enjoy teaching after initial nervousness and did so for over twenty years, then I started to concentrate on research; at Hatfield I was lecturing to a group of about ten to fifteen for tutorials but when I came here I was lecturing to 80-120 people whom I wouldn't see again unless they were in my College and I was supervising them; felt more detached from the students when lecturing

43:46:08 When I came here I was very ignorant about Cambridge as I wasn't here as an undergraduate; Roger Needham suggested that I might go to Newnham where I became an Unofficial Fellow, but I also directed studies for New Hall and Lucy Cavendish; over the years I realized there were very few women students in computer science, and very few of them in the women's colleges; in the end there were no students at all at Newnham so I moved to Pembroke to direct studies; in 1997 I moved to Jesus as a Fellow; I have always taught computing, not mathematics; I enjoy supervising and still do it; I do still lecture although it is a bit of an ordeal; I do a lot of external professional service and committees; are you being asked as a token woman or do they really want you there is a thought, but those I have done I felt that I was there in my own right; in College I was quite old when I went there so tended to be put on appeals committees, for example; quite enjoy these; we all grumble about box ticking and process which has expanded over the years

47:07:21 I got my PhD in 1981; I got a research grant at a time when not many people were aware of how to get grants; I started to go to workshops at the Science and Engineering Research Council where everyone working in distributed computing came together; good for me as Hatfield was very much orientated on teaching; it gave me the confidence to think of moving on; I applied for jobs at both Cambridge and University College, London, and got both; then I had to decide whether commuting from Watford to London or Cambridge was easier; decided to come to Cambridge as I had always rather regretted not coming here as an undergraduate; I had met Cambridge people throughout my career - at NPL, GEC; Jim Wilkinson at NPL was at Trinity, and I kept coming across brilliant mathematicians from Cambridge which made me realize what a good place it was rather than just a place for public school children which I had not really understood when I was at school; I had not met similarly brilliant Oxford mathematicians so Cambridge began to feel special; at school I did feel it would be difficult to fit in but also I had been in the sixth form long enough and didn't want to spend a fourth year to take the Cambridge scholarship; when I came here I did not feel uncomfortable at all and that places like King's had had student from northern grammar schools for years; at the last school reunion someone mentioned that when interviewing for languages at Oxford, she felt the other students were much better prepared than she was; it may be that mathematics and computing are different; on colleges - I ended up at Jesus where the Master was David Crighton, then Robert Mair, both mathematicians/engineers; I overlapped a little with Colin Renfrew

53:00:07 When I came to Cambridge I was still working on distributed systems and operating systems at the lower level, and rather less as the years went by; I had a project in filing systems which might have distributed components; multimedia was just beginning with related processing and storage issue; we had realized that the software must communicate so the source of any communication was always a software component; then we got to a stage where we were monitoring the environment where unpredictable things happen; this has moved on to sensors monitoring the environment, medical sensors monitoring people's health, traffic monitoring; we have moved to the paradigm where the events are coming from outside the computer system and we have got to respond to them, so it is what is called an asynchronous paradigm instead of just components interacting; a different thread that my group has worked on is access control; we have worked with medics on how you specify who should see what data; the special thing about health care data is that its sensitivity persists for a lifetime or longer; for cancer records, they are not just confidential for a day but indefinitely; you have to worry about how it is encrypted, whether it gets transferred in the encrypted form, and how long the keys are going to be secure; maybe you don't even send all the data outside where it lives; you must know which records relate to the same person but not allow anyone to see who that person is outside the one place where the records are held; on the recent scandals over lost data - we have always known that the highest bandwidth way of transferring data was on a disc, now a memory stick, but both these and laptops are vulnerable to human error or theft; there is no way of preventing this as it is a human problem; it is very scary the amount of data that is being collected on us and there can be no assurances that it can be held securely as the human element is the weakness; I suppose that all the material must be encrypted and not allowed to go onto laptops in any other form; the recent cases were human error but industrial espionage is all too easy

58:24:07 Roger Needham was head of department when I came to Cambridge, and he and his wife Karen were very kind when I first came; Karen's main work was in natural language processing and information retrieval, which came into its own when the web was invented in the early 1990's; I had not associated Cambridge with information retrieval before I came; [In the interview here I say that the main work I was aware of in IR before coming to Cambridge was a book by Salton from Cranfield.

This is wrong. Cyril Cleverdon worked on the Cranfield collection,

Gerard Salton was Professor of Computer Science at Cornell, developed the SMART IR system and wrote Automatic Information Organization and Retrieval in 1968];

Keith van Rijsbergen's probabilistic approach to information retrieval is important, as is Martin Porter's work, but it is not my area; I did work with one natural language MPhil student as we did need to know how to express who should access health records, and we did work with Steve Pullman using discourse diagrams and first order logic to generate code from pseudo-natural language; Maurice Wilkes was Roger's predecessor; he is extremely courteous and has always been nice to me, a good organizer and a brilliant lecturer; he started the Diploma here, which was the first Computing course in the world; he has just given the final set of diploma certificates out; it is a pity that is has finished but the Government wanted Masters training programmes rather than conversion courses, but our Diploma course has converted so many wonderful mathematicians, physicists and scientists of all kinds to computing that it has done an enormous service; five years ago we lost the twenty odd studentships and the course has declined since then; Wilkes was a pioneer but he has kept going and is still lecturing; David Wheeler was the same, very nice and supportive, a brilliant mathematician; Andy Hopper is a brilliant head of department, full of energy and inventiveness; out of his research group has come location technology including such things as active badges which can monitor where you are; we have interacted with clinical and biomedical computing but not much with spin-off companies; I have never come across problems of conflict of interest; we make our software developed from research grants available on our web site to people who want to use it

1:09:17:00 Ken Moody and I work on the same research projects; he was interested in databases but also in distributed systems, so there was an overlap in interests; over the years we have got research grants together and our interests coincided rather more as time went by; he is a good theoretician so can give the theory courses; he has kept up maths and always does the maths exam papers before they are given to students; we got together as much through me trying to find nature reserves when I came to Cambridge as through the overlap in research interests; I also needed somewhere to paint, and King's had a studio; I have always tried to find time to paint, and when I came to Cambridge I found that King's had an art teacher cum artist in residence; I worked with Hermione Holmes then Rose Rands; at that stage I had never had exhibitions but Rose encouraged me; I had something to really work for; think that it is a great idea and gives you confidence; Ken has always been interested in photography; he now photographs flowers because of my interest in them; the reed bed project over the last three years has been a joint project; we had moved to Suffolk near the coast where there are reed beds which are wonderful throughout the year; I asked him to photograph them and he did so all through 2005 and I started the painting project after that

1:14:12:12 Have another two years before official retirement; I have a new research grant starting in October and have two new PhD students which is a three year commitment; I very much enjoy research; it has been such a privilege to work with bright young academics as post docs and young lecturers and I think I would miss that terribly; I have supervised thirty-seven PhD's in all; I always worry about them but I think that getting jobs for them is not a problem; one of the exciting things that is happening at the moment is the fact that a single computer is a multiprocessor; I have always worked in concurrency control, and this is coming into its own because instead of working with a single processor per computer with memory you are now going to always have multiple computer processors, and you need to exploit that; the concurrency issue may mean that they are interfering with each other's data; this is a problem that has to be solved; in Suffolk we have no television or internet, just lots of music and walking

Keith van Rijsbergen

15 July 2009

http://downloads.sms.cam.ac.uk/1129910/1129917.mp4

C. J. van Rijsbergen, Fabio Crestani and Mouia Laimas,
Information Retrieval: Uncertainty and Logics (1998)

C. J. "Keith" van Rijsbergen (Cornelis Joost van Rijsbergen) (born 1943) is a professor of computer science and the leader of the Glasgow Information Retrieval Group based at the University of Glasgow. He is one of the founders of modern Information Retrieval and the author of the seminal monograph *Information Retrieval* and of the textbook *The Geometry of Information Retrieval.*

He was born near Rotterdam, and educated in the Netherlands, Indonesia, Namibia and Australia. His first degree is in mathematics from the University of Western Australia, and in 1972 he completed a PhD in computer science at the University of Cambridge. He spent three years lecturing in information retrieval and artificial intelligence at Monash University before returning to Cambridge to hold a Royal Society Information Research Fellowship. In 1980 he was appointed to the chair of computer science at University College Dublin; from there he moved in 1986 to Glasgow University. In 2003 he was inducted as a Fellow of the Association for Computing Machinery. In 2004 he was awarded the Tony Kent Strix award. In 2006, he was awarded the Gerard Salton Award for *Quantum haystacks.* Since 2007 he has been Chairman of the Scientific Board of the Information Retrieval Facility.

INTERVIEW SUMMARY

Keith van Rijsbergen interviewed by Alan Macfarlane 15th July 2009

0:09:07 Born near Rotterdam in Holland in 1943; my memory kicks in at the end of the War; I remember my family parading in the street celebrating, although whether it was a memory given to me by my mother or I actually remembered, I have no idea; my father had quite a bad war; he was an engineer and he was on the run from the Germans; they wanted him to build things to do with their defences, and he refused; he was finally caught and sent to a prisoner-of-war camp on the Polish-East German border; some years ago when the wall came down I went and visited the place but the camp was gone; our life after the war was quite complicated as my father travelled a lot as an engineer and took the family with him; we left Holland for the first time about 1949 and we went to Indonesia; between 1945 and 1949 he had done some major construction work on the harbours in Rotterdam which I have records of; my brother, sister, and I, with our mother followed my father to Indonesia three months after, and settled in Jakarta; father doing work on the harbour; we lived right in the centre of Jakarta very close to a famous river called the Kali, and our neighbour was Sukarno; he lived in a huge house and we lived in something like a hotel; I went to school there; about ten years ago I met a fellow computer scientist, a Dutch man, and found that we had been in the same primary school in Jakarta; my father stayed in Indonesia for about three or four years; during that time we moved around and spent time in Surabaya, also in Java, some time in Borneo, and also Sumatra; in all these places I went to school and learnt to speak Indonesian as did my brother and sister; we conversed in the language but some years after we had left, completely forgot the language; the memory of that time is still strong because it was like an adventure; I was completely free to roam around in and out of the jungle, so a very happy memory; I have never been back although I have wanted to

6:33:03 My father was a quiet type; occasionally he would lose his temper and hit us, but not in a severe way; most people would say I was not very close to him but he looms because it was his activities that determined where we went and what we did; my mother was an extremely nervous person; she almost had a nervous breakdown having to follow my father to Indonesia; this was displayed in huge arguments with her children; as the youngest I was more of an observer but she certainly upset the others; however, the relationship between my mother and myself was actually quite close; she was always at home, my father worked twelve hours a day, so she was quite influential in many ways; she always gave us, particularly me, a lot of freedom to do what we wanted, providing we told her what we were doing and when we would be back; none of the family actually finished school or were academically inclined; my mother only went to primary school, father only had three years of high school and my brother and sister similarly; I was the only one who was academically inclined and my parents did not understand this and tried to encourage me just to get a job

9:47:09 I start to remember things about school from the age of about fourteen-fifteen, prior to that I have virtually no memory of school, certainly not Indonesia; I can recall going to school and leaving it, and doing things out of school, but have no memory of anything in it; realized I was quite good at mathematics when I was going to high school but there were no signs of this before; after Indonesia we went back to Holland; this was a recurring pattern; the next contract was in Western Australia and we lived on the outskirts of Perth; I went to a normal primary school and have a bit more memory of this as it was there that I learned to speak English; when I first arrived at the school the teacher told another boy to take me outside and teach me the alphabet; that is the only thing that I remember about learning English, the rest was by a sort of osmosis; my parents attitude was that wherever we were, the children should go to the local school, whatever the language, and just get on with it; I don't remember anything traumatic about not being able to speak English; at that school they discovered that I was quite good at maths and science; after about a year and a half they pushed me on and I was put into first year high school a year before I should have been; however it didn't help much as we soon after left to go back to Holland; I have some minor memories of living in Perth, a little of school, but more of biking to the beach and spending time swimming; in winter I would spend time walking in the bush with a friend; a lot of my time was spent outside; I did read a lot but it didn't interfere with my outdoor life; the school was Hilton Park Primary School and I remember a teacher by the name of Simpson; many years later I bumped into him in Fremantle although he didn't remember me; I think I remember him for his kindness and not for being a good teacher; at that stage I don't have much of a memory of teachers being good or bad; I remember them being more or less violent as they still caned people, but he was rather a kind person; while we were in Western Australia the Queen visited, probably in 1953, and came to the school, and I remember that as a big occasion, but the strongest memory I have is of swimming

16:00:00 Our walks in the bush were not systematic; we were not collecting things but pretending to be Cowboys and Indians; the bush was on the edge of where we lived so I only had to cross the road to it; it was not particularly dangerous and we went barefoot; we then left Australia and again went back to Holland; from a school point of view this was quite a critical moment; I think we may have lived with my grandmother for a while; because I had just gone to the high school in Fremantle I was then put into a high school in Dordrecht; it was called the MULO which is a school which teaches children useful things so they can go into commerce; at that school they discovered that I was quite bright academically; it was recommended to my parents that I be sent to the HBS which is like a Gymnasium and streams children for university; that is where my interest in science and mathematics took off; I had to get some extra coaching in mathematics to catch up; I realized that I was rather good at physics as well; we went back to live in the place where I was born; that was where I grew to love going to the cinema, read a lot but mostly light stuff, and continued swimming

19:56:01 Started to wear glasses in Australia just before going to high school; I remember feeling quite shy at having to wear them but don't remember it persisting; I was not a keen games player, but my favourite sport was swimming; always felt other games were constraining; I was not a great team player; I was quite rebellious; in Holland I was actually suspended from school for a few days but can't remember why; I probably was slightly resentful of authority, not being allowed to do the things that I wanted to do, and this led me into trouble; in Australia I used to go around pinching fruit from orchards; back in Holland in what I thought was a reasonable education system, I was also taught French and German; the Dutch system in those days was very extensive; I think I had about seventeen subjects, and they were done to quite a reasonable standard; one of my memories of that period is that I went to the World Exhibition in Brussels, in about 1957; just before that the Sputnik had been put into space and the Russians had a display model at the exhibition; there were also displays of, what were then, modern technologies; I remember seeing the first colour television set in the American pavilion; we had family in Brussels and used to visit them quite regularly; my father came from a very large family and some of his brothers lived in Belgium; my mother came from quite a small family and her father was a market gardener; she had a brother and sister; she did not keep up much contact with her family; I still have contact with my father's family, but not in Holland

25:47:19 The next stage in my father's career was to go to what was then called South West Africa, Namibia; this was the last three years of high school; we lived in a town called Walvis Bay on the coast; the school was in Swakopmund about forty miles away; I travelled there every day by bus; although the school was Afrikaans and English a lot of the kids were German, so I learned to speak German simply by osmosis; I read a lot in German and Swakopmund had a very good bookshop; one of the books that influenced me in the direction of science was Fred Hoyle's book 'The Frontiers of Astronomy' which I read in German; that was when I started to look a books that had serious scientific content; I read Rutherford on the atom and Eddington's 'Nature of the Physical World'; I was also reading literature including Dostoyevsky; I saw myself as part of the beatnik generation though probably all it meant was wearing a floppy sweater; it was the time that academic-type reading became more important; I continued to swim despite a cold current which comes up from the Antarctic along the west coast of Namibia which makes the water very cold;

there is a pier in Swakopmund that goes out into the sea and I used to swim around it every day; again, a lot of my memories are of things I did outside school; in my holidays I worked on a fishing boat; in the summer the boat would function as a trawler and I worked as a deckhand, sorting fish; in winter it was converted to catch pilchards by net, and that was a night activity; another thing I remember well was going up-country, hunting with a friend whose parents had a farm; I spent quite a lot of time walking round the desert near where we lived; in terms of friends, in Namibia at Swakopmund I made a very good friend whom I remained in contact with for quite a few years afterwards; the friends I made before that I did not keep in contact with for long; as a family we also went on vacation in South Africa; we had a Land Rover so would drive down to Cape Town and Durban, so we saw quite a lot of the country; towards the end of our stay in Namibia I was in a major train crash; I was on the way to visit my brother in Durban and there was a head-on collision with another train; I was in the front coach; the engine went straight through the coach and smashed its way through until it got to my compartment; all those in front were killed; I crawled out of the wreckage virtually unharmed; I had the presence of mind to take photographs and then walked off to the nearest road, hitched a ride and continued my journey

34:41:24 On religious background, my parents inherited their parents' religion which was fairly protestant Calvinist; there was a moment when I was six or seven that they said that I didn't have to say grace before a meal if I didn't want to; I think that they had lost their religion; I think I decided I was not religious about the age of fourteen; I had no desire to go to church and didn't personally think that I believed in God; Martin Rees once said that he was a non-believing Christian and I think that that is quite close to what I am; I understand and accept the culture that we have has come out of Christianity, but that doesn't mean to say that I also have to believe in God; when I was a teenager in Namibia I read a lot of Spinoza and that must have had an impact on me as well; there were things I read that made me become more sceptical about religion; my wife is the daughter of an Anglican Vicar and that made me take an intellectual interest in theology; I am not like Richard Dawkins, I don't feel antagonistic towards religion; if people want to believe that is fine; I actually enjoy having proper theological arguments; the other thing that happened in Namibia was that I stayed on for my last year of school, on my own; my parents went back to Holland but they arranged for me to be accommodated in a maternity home which had rooms that were rented out; when I had first arrived in Namibia my parents had enquired about an appropriate school for me; the headmaster determined that as I did not speak Afrikaans I would have to learn it; they decided that I should go into a hostel at the school; unfortunately I was not very popular because I had made a lot of English/German friends and there was antagonism between them and the Afrikaners; every few days I would have a fight on my hands having to defend myself; eventually I got fed up; I rang my mother and told her I was coming home; they must have realized that it was serious; the school decided I could stay although I had not really learned enough Afrikaans; at the end of my time at that school you had to take not only your leaving certificate but also a certificate in English and Afrikaans; I decided that the mathematics at school was poor and I explained this to my parents; they suggested that I signed up for a Dutch correspondence course, which I did, and this brought my mathematics up to a standard that went beyond what was offered by the school; I think that from going to school there I got my love of languages and literature; languages, especially English literature, was taught to quite a high standard and we were expected to read quite a lot; the English literature teacher was one of the people that I remember very well, and I liked; he was a rather unusual person who would invite me to his house and I would play chess with him; I think he must have realized that I was academically inclined because he always encouraged me

43:48:10 I had enrolled to go to university in Natal to study mathematics and had got a scholarship to do that; my parents then wrote to me to say that they were going back to Australia and were coming to collect me on their way; we met in Durban where my brother was; my sister had already gone back to Australia; with them and my brother we went by a cargo vessel to Australia; I was again moved to another education system and it was not as straightforward as they had said it would be; it turned out that the University of Western Australia didn't recognise my qualifications;

they agreed to let me start provisionally while trying to get my qualifications accredited; about two-thirds of the way through my first year they agreed finally that I could stay; I wanted to do physics and philosophy as well as mathematics; the University would not allow philosophy so I started to do physics, chemistry, pure mathematics and applied mathematics; I felt this a bit of a compromise as I wanted more than just pure science; I had quite a lot of catching up to do in some aspects; no sooner had I started my course than my parents left and went to the east coast of Australia; once again I was left on my own; I learned that I left South Africa at the same time as David King, in 1962; he left for political reasons and I realize that in my three months in Durban I was becoming politically aware; up to that point although I was aware of Apartheid and that it was questionable, it was not a big issue; when I was in Durban I got to meet some of the students and they were fairly political; I went to some of Athol Fugard's plays, one I remember clearly was 'Blood Knot' which was closed down almost as soon as I had seen it; I started to get concerned so maybe it was quite a good thing that I was leaving South Africa; talking to David, although he was more advanced in his thinking at that time, we were struggling with the same thing

49:14:24 My mother at that stage had calmed down; one of the things that had happened in Indonesia which was perhaps one of the reasons she was extremely nervous, was that my father was nearly murdered twice; he was in charge of people on the engineering site and for some reason they decided to run him over with a truck and left him for dead; he recovered, but no sooner was he out of hospital than they tried to kill him again, with knives; at that time there was a lot of tension between the Dutch and Indonesians because the latter was becoming independent and the Dutch were the old colonial masters; my mother just didn't believe that my father was going to die so she stayed with him in hospital and he recovered; when we were back in South Africa and took the boat to Australia I remember her as being quite calm and at ease with herself; when studying I met my wife, Juliet; we met in the mathematics lecture theatre and because we were both short-sighted we had to sit in the front; we went through our first degree together and married in 1965 at about the time we graduated; I did not like the formal education that I was getting, and resented the canned, limited and boring way in which they presented stuff to us; I thus spent a lot of my time getting books out of the library and reading around subjects; I would take notes in lectures but would burn them at the end of the year as quite useless; I seemed to have an approach to science that I had to get the story in my head that at other times I could think about the stuff; it was not enough to just have the proof; in mathematics they would, for example, give a lecture on the Hahn-Banach theorem, then meticulously go through the proof on the blackboard; this did not work for my and I found it totally uninteresting; I had to go away and read about the Hahn-Banach theorem, and how it fitted into other bits of mathematics; maybe even read about the people involved, so for me always my interest in science was added to by knowing about the people who were doing it; before I came to university I had already read and understood the special theory of relativity, but at the same time I had found out a lot about Einstein; I wanted to do theoretical physics because of this; the physics department in Western Australia had a strong experimental component and I found it boring; you had to stand doing experiments in the afternoon, and they would take three hours; at that stage suffered very badly from migraines, particularly when standing for long periods; this wiped out the rest of the day; I told the Professor of Physics and asked if I could do just theoretical physics; he said I couldn't do just theoretical physics so suggested I focussed on applied mathematics; that is what I did; it was a strange period because I think the University worked their students very hard but I felt they did not instil any excitement about the subject during the lectures, and did not motivate us well; the dropout rate in mathematics was very high so although I started with a large cohort, by the time I got to the end very few were left; I thought I was not going to make it because when I was tested by a psychologist in my first year he said that I was totally unsuited for university work; I think it may have had something to do with my command of English at that point as I had been speaking German or Afrikaans; the thing that I remember most about university is finding these wonderful things to read in the library; that is how I learned a lot of stuff I had to learn, lectures just didn't work for me; my wife seems to think I did the right thing as she just concentrated on the lecture notes and now retains nothing of that stuff, whereas I have retained the story

Second Part

0:07:09 I did not have a scholarship so I had to pay my own way; I worked as a crayfisherman, a weighbridge officer, an assistant electrician, in an auction room, as a quantity surveyor, so had a string of experiences in different types of jobs; by this means I paid most of my way through university; at the same time my relationship with my wife went from strength to strength and we are still here; after graduating we decided that we wanted to leave Western Australia and go back to Europe; before doing so, with a degree in mathematics, felt I needed a meal ticket; I therefore enrolled for a year in a diploma course on numerical analysis and automatic computing; thus I retrained as a computing person; surprisingly I discovered that I liked it; my wife, also with a degree in mathematics, took a diploma of education; we got on a boat with a number of other graduates and came to England; before setting off I wrote to a number of places in England with computing centres asking for a job; I did not come here with the intention to do a PhD; a letter was sent to the Computing Service in Cambridge; Eric Mutch was the head of the service but he had no job to offer but he contacted Nick Jardine; they thought they might be able to offer me a job as a programmer; I arrived in 1969 and was interviewed by Nick Jardine in King's; he said he could give me part-time employment but that the Computer Lab could also offer some work; Nick had a project with Robin Sibson, who was also in King's at that time; they had just finished their PhDs on automatic classification in the biological sciences; Eric Mutch died soon after I arrived, but I continued in the lab working on a sub-routine library in numerical analysis which ran for many years on TITAN; after working for about nine months I told Nick that I was getting very bored; he suggested I do a PhD; the idea I had for it grew out of the work I was doing for Nick and Robin in the King's College Research Centre, which was to try and use automatic classification techniques in information retrieval; I had an interest in information retrieval even before I left Australia so had already read about it when I arrived in Cambridge; I put these things together and this was how I got to know Karen Sparck Jones; King's College was going to have me as a research student and subsidise my fees; I remember assuming that I could do a PhD in information retrieval providing I was not supervised by Karen Sparck Jones; Ken Moody who at that stage had an interest in databases took me on; I think that was a stroke of genius because I collaborated with Karen all along but it was not a student-supervisor arrangement; she was generous in giving me access to the test data she had but was not my supervisor; I also got a lot of help from Roger Needham

9:06:08 The history of information retrieval in Cambridge is quite interesting; Roger Needham, a famous computer scientist in a totally different area, did his PhD in information retrieval; I suspect that it was the first PhD ever done on that subject; he was supervised by David Wheeler who is one of the pioneers, and worked with Maurice Wilkes; there was a progression David to Roger who, to a certain extent, helped me; Nick and Robin had conversations with Roger with their work in automatic classification because he and Karen worked together in the Cambridge Language Research Unit on the theory of clumps; I think that Karen got her initial ideas about information retrieval probably from Roger; Karen came in as a linguist where she had done her PhD work, which apparently, even now, is still read and considered to be very good; it was on synonyms; her thesis was republished recently under pressure from Yorick Wilks; he was also a member of the Cambridge Language Research Unit, which also had Fred Parker-Rhodes, who may also have done some work on information retrieval, and also Margaret Masterman; the group that I knew worked on language and linguistics and shaded into stuff on information retrieval; when I was starting to work for Nick and Robin there was this huge intellectual disagreement between them and the Needhams because the clumping process was considered to be very unprincipled, whereas the approach adopted by Jardine and Sibson, later Jardine & Sibson 'Mathematical Taxonomy', was considered very principled and mathematically well defined; as it turned out the algorithms or methods of automatic classification that came out of their work was relatively efficient, whereas clumping was horribly inefficient; what happened in the end was that the Jardine-Sibson work that turned into my work too, survived, whereas the clumping didn't; I was caught between these two groups but I had my office in the Research Centre where at the same time Denis Mollison, a probabilist, was also working; his application was pandemics so had mathematical models for the current flu pandemic; he became Professor of Statistics at Heriot-Watt and was on the fringes of our project; the other person who was quite involved with the project was Ken Moody; I don't know whether he was officially written into the project proposal but he was certainly acting as a consultant; he designed the original algorithm for a sequence of cluster methods called BK, the core of which was based on his work; as a supervisor he took an interest in what I was doing when it really mattered; I was an appalling writer to begin with, it was so condensed that if I was to write the same stuff now, one paragraph would take several pages; Ken got me to think about how to write; I went on to do my PhD thesis on automatic classification techniques; I tested them to show that if used in the way that I did, at least on the data that I had, it showed that you could get major performance increase; on the way I also invented an evaluation measure which is used to this day, in fact is used very widely in speech recognition, so was adopted by another field as a measure of retrieval performance; it was some of the theoretical work that I really enjoyed doing; I went back to some theory called the theory of measurement that suggests that if you want to measure something where the objects are in a qualitative relationship, what you have to do is to define a mapping of these to a numerical representation where properties of the qualitative structure are preserved; I took that approach to measuring performance in information retrieval; I wrote down the intuitive conditions or relationships that were important in IR and the ones that you wanted to measure, and then defined this mapping; I came up with this new way of measuring things and it has persisted; it is still used in information retrieval and also in speech processing; so automatic classification, the method and the algorithms for IR and this evaluation technique were really the guts of my thesis; Karen, who really was not mathematical on the whole, helped me with the linguistic stuff; she was the one who explained to me about stemming and stop words, and the way it was driven by some background in linguistics; she had also built up some test collections and she allowed me to use them; our interactions were mostly around the experimental side of information retrieval

19:02:06 While I was doing my PhD, my wife taught at a number of schools, especially Impington Village College, and after a difficult first six months in Cambridge we ended up being happy here; Maurice Wilkes only entered my life towards the end of my PhD; he really didn't see the point of information retrieval; I thought that information retrieval should be a subject in the computer science curriculum and he never really allowed that; I think Karen half agreed but was ambiguous about whether she wanted it as part of a computer science degree; she had quite an interesting attitude to IR; she saw it very much as a post graduate activity but then she took very few PhD students; she had one, David Jackson, who preceded me, and after that there was a huge gap; what she did do was to supervise students in natural language processing; she did supervise Martin Porter but in macro processors; there was a language called Snowbol, and he designed and invented a comparable language; he was a superb software engineer; Martin came into our lives when I came back again from Australia; after I took my PhD I was head-hunted by the Professor of Computer Science at Monash University in Melbourne; his name was Chris Wallace and he worked on automatic classification; he was a good, able, academic, but it was different from the automatic classification work that people did here; we went out to Monash and there our daughter, Nicola, was born five months after we arrived; however, as a lecturer in computer science I got very bored; I had nobody to talk to really about information retrieval; I had the idea of talking to myself and wrote a book about it; the book did well and is still used to this day; half-way through my contractual period I returned to Cambridge to try and figure out if there was a way that I could come back; Karen suggested I apply for a Royal Society Research Fellowship which I did; I got it, so after two and a half years in Monash, I came back to Cambridge and bought a house

24:56:16 Academically there was a development going on in information retrieval which turned out to be extremely significant, in fact theoretically probably one of the most important in the subject; there are various models for information retrieval; the standard one, probably the oldest, what we call a vector space model, researched by Gerard Salton at Cornell; the sense was that there was enough uncertainty in information retrieval processes that we had to use probabilistic approaches; the first major development in that area was a thesis written by an academic, Bill Miller, at Newcastle University; he invented a new model - probabilistic retrieval as it is now called; the trouble was that it was only half a model; Karen working with Stephen Robertson but he was in danger of not having a job; we worked out a way of employing him as a research assistant; on that project we also employed Martin Porter as another research assistant; he was working on probabilistic models for our project so the suffix stripping algorithm, called the Porter Algorithm, was invented on the project; I gave him the task of building one and he did a fantastic job; he went and read all the literature on such algorithms on the linguistic side and computing side, then he put it all together and produced this algorithm; it is still used; any information retrieval experiment that is done, even with commercial systems, they tend to use the Porter Algorithm; Martin was not really a researcher, more of a developer, writing the software and building a system; he and Karen did not get on so one of the problems we had on the project was that every so often we would need something from Karen and then she would give him a hard time; he was not good at coping with that; Karen was very forthright and Martin didn't like to be hassled, so got very upset; Stephen, who was going to be on the project, at the last moment got a job so he became the co-investigator with me, so we employed Martin; I think he is a brilliant software engineer, one of the best I know in terms of getting things done; I was on the fringes of Muscat; he took an earlier system that he had written for the Museum Documentation people and extended it, as I saw it, with some information retrieval functionality; some of that he probably got from working with myself earlier on

31:24:10 My relationship with Maurice Wilkes got better when I became interested in Alan Turing; Maurice is very aware of his position in the history of computer science, and rightly so; he is one of the founders and pioneers, and certainly you can make the argument that, with David Wheeler etc., he built the first real computer, the EDSAC; Alan Turing, especially at the moment, but certainly towards the end of the 1970s, became more well known for his work; at that time the Scientific Archives in Oxford rang King's and said they had papers by a man called Turing who seemed to be originally from King's; they asked if King's could send someone to say whether they were worth preserving; the Librarian, Peter Crofts, asked me to go and look at them; like everybody else I had heard of a Turing Machine but I knew little more than that about him; I saw the papers and suggested they were brought to King's; progressively King's got more and more serious about them and I later got some money to help with them; at that time most people would not have heard of him but I talked to Maurice Wilkes at some time and he clearly felt that Turing was being given too much prominence in the history of things; you can see that from his point of view, Alan Turing was a theoretician and wrote this incredibly smart paper in the 1930s on the Entscheidungsproblem; he spent the War at Bletchley Park involved in the design of computers - (not the Colossus, that had nothing to do with him) ; after the war, when working at the NPL, he wrote the ACE Report, a blueprint for designing a computer which was in contrast to a similar report written by John von Neumann which was the EDVAC Report; the EDVAC was the first complete design for a computer and Turing's came a little later; Wilkes, on the other hand, started to think about building EDSAC and got his information from the same sources as von Neumann and Turing; Eckert and Mauchly who gave courses in the Moore School of Electrical Engineering, University of Pennsylvania, were the source of new ideas about a modern computer; Wilkes's attitude was that he was just going to build it, and as an engineer that is what he did; he tried to collaborate with Turing but they didn't like each other; the EDSAC was built and was a success; the ACE machine was only built very much later in the 1950s, so its impact on the design of the next generation of machines was not very significant; however, I think that Maurice sees Turing as unjustifiably getting more support than he ought to because his work was theoretical and as far as building the computer, his engineering skills were not great; nowadays everybody has heard of Turing because of the books and films which Wilkes would feel overstates what he actually accomplished; I am a great admirer of Turing but more for his theoretical work; I think his thoughts on the Turing Machine were an incredible breakthrough but his contribution to the actual building of computers is nowhere near as significant as Maurice's are; Winston Churchill said that we were saved from a German invasion by him but in a letter to him, I think Churchill said that it had shortened the War by about a year; Turing started work on encrypting using his theoretical knowledge, so the bombe, the mechanical devise to do the decoding was based on the theoretical ideas Turing had at Bletchley Park; after that early period he was not working on that any more; he got moved onto speech encryption; the work that led to the Colossus was independent, and Turing was only on the edge of that; his story was very sad; he moved to Manchester and worked in the computer laboratory there; he was forced to undergo drug treatment because of his homosexuality; the book his mother wrote about him is a delight to read; I have interviewed Maurice about Turing as I wanted to know whether he had read the ACE Report about the design of a modern computer; Maurice claims he did not read it and worked independently of Turing

42:45:17 I was at Monash at the time that Stephen and Karen were working on probability; I also made the shift in my mind and had a student build a probabilistic search engine as a student project; my approach to it was slightly different; I took a decision theoretic approach so developed some sort of decision theory, so when Karen and Stephen produced their draft paper and sent it to me, I reworked it in decision theoretic terms which is I still think a good way to do it; there was a kind of debate going on between the three of us about how to formulate it; some people would say that the probabilistic model (which I wrote about in the second edition of my book) was actually developed by the three of us; however, if I am honest I certainly think that I probably had the same ideas to the same extent; the paper that was published by Karen and Stephen is the first publication of that work although it has a subset in it which is on the decision theoretic approach; in the other way that I was in the thick of it was that I started building, together with Martin, implementations of it; for example, the relevance feedback comes out of that model; I was much more interested to get it working at that stage than to define the theory; like a lot of these things, it is very difficult to pinpoint where the breakthroughs were made; there was this earlier thesis by the Bill Miller from Newcastle, who actually ended up in Glasgow University, who had a pretty good formal development of it, but he didn't seriously take into account the non-occurrence of things, thus it was half a model; it was completed in the paper by Karen and Stephen; I should have had my name on that, but I didn't

47:21:15 I don't have great thoughts sitting at a computer terminal; to this day I still hand-write important stuff first and not at home; I am one of these people who actually works in cafes; most of my papers were drafted by hand in a notebook in a cafe somewhere; I worked for a long time in the old 'Copper Kettle', and I wasn't the only person that did; Green, who contributed much to string theory, was working in another corner, though at that time I had no idea who he was; I used to get ideas in the bath and when cycling; it would be unusual for me to sort something out sitting at my desk staring at a blank piece of paper or a screen; I can't sit still for very long either; if I work for an hour and a half I then have to go for a walk anyway, I am a restless researcher

50:35:03 I enjoy music, particularly singing and jazz; my background meant that none of my siblings or parents played any musical instrument; until the age of sixteen there was not a record player in the house; my mother and father were pretty much a-musical; my brother liked to play the mouth organ but was exposed in the same way to not having any music in the house; I only discovered music gradually, I absolutely adore opera and am a great fan of jazz, especially blues; I use music as a way of relaxing; I used to take a bath to do that; now if I come home shattered, I put on a piece of music - recently Handel's 'Julius Caesar' - and I just listen to the whole opera; my wife and I share the same taste in music so wherever we go we try to go to performances as I also enjoy the staging; I also read a huge amount of fiction both in English and in Dutch; again it is a way of escaping from the technical stuff that I do

55:09:17 I have supervised about thirty PhD students and about 60% of them are now full professors around the world; in my supervisions what I try to do is to engineer one thing; I want them to have the central idea themselves, they should come up with it if the possibly can, although I might stimulate it, but then I want them to end up owning it; then when I start to argue with them they show clear signs that it is their idea; once they have reached that point then they are well on the way; how do you do that? I say that they should follow their noses, and choose to do something they are interested in and want to do, not something that they were just told to do; it seems to work although I have had students where it has not, and generally they don't do as well in terms of a career afterwards; I believe in the academic way of life and have enjoyed it immensely; the thing that I have resented in the last ten to fifteen years is the extent to which the bureaucracy in universities have started to drive things; they create circumstances which academics have to respond to which are basically just stopping you from doing the intellectual work; it is not that I feel that academics should just do intellectual work, but the burden of doing the non-intellectual work, dealing with either national or local bureaucracy, has become rather over-excessive and I think very sad; my daughter is an academic, a post doc in neuroscience, and I can see that the pressure is there already on her to cope with bureaucratic excesses

Ben Shneiderman

7 August 2009

http://downloads.sms.cam.ac.uk/1130395/1130402.mp4

Ben Shneiderman, *Leonardo's Laptop: Human Needs and the New Computing Technologies* (2002)

Ben Shneiderman is an American computer scientist, and professor for Computer Science at the University of Maryland Human-Computer Interaction Lab at the University of Maryland, College Park. He conducted fundamental research in the field of human–computer interaction, developing new ideas, methods, and tools such as the direct manipulation interface, and his eight rules of design.

In his earlier work on studying programmers, he conducted experiments which suggested that flowcharts were not helpful for writing, understanding, or modifying computer programs. He developed the principles of Direct manipulation interface design in 1982, and applied this to develop the user interface for highlighted phrases in text, that became the hot link of the Web. In 1986, he published the first edition (now on its fifth edition) of his book "Designing the User Interface: Strategies for Effective Human-Computer Interaction." Included in this book is his most popular list of "Eight Golden Rules of Interface Design".

His major work in recent years has been on information visualization, originating the treemap concept for hierarchical data. He also developed dynamic queries sliders with multiple coordinated displays that are a key component of Spotfire, which was acquired by TIBCO in 2007. His work continued on visual analysis tools for time series data, TimeSearcher, high dimensional data, Hierarchical Clustering Explorer, and social network data, SocialAction plus NodeXL.

Current work deals with visualization of temporal event sequences, such as found in Electronic Health Records, in systems such as LifeLines2.

In addition to his influential work in user interface design, he is known for the co-invention (together with Isaac Nassi) of the Nassi–Shneiderman diagrams, a graphical representation of the design of structured software.

He also defined the research area of universal usability to encourage greater attention to diverse users, languages, cultures, screen sizes, network speeds, and technology platforms.

INTERVIEW SUMMARY

Ben Shneiderman interviewed by Alan Macfarlane 7th August 2009

0:09:07 Born 1947 in New York City; grew up in a warm environment with parents and a sister who had been born in Paris in 1937; my parents came to New York in February 1940 to escape the oncoming war; I was born after all the turbulence and loss; all four of my grandparents were killed in the Warsaw Ghetto; the community of family that I had when growing up in Manhattan, surrounded by other cousins, was very important to me; I appreciated the environment my parents created as journalists involved in the Jewish community and the New York literary world; they wrote later about their homeland, Poland, and Eastern Europe; my parents used to write together, my father dictating and mother transcribing; my father would cut and paste with glue and scissors many times, and then my mother would retype; I don't have trouble writing as I know how difficult it is; it is difficult because people have a desire to make it perfect on the first try, and to do so takes much reworking; remember Winston Churchill's comment that he would practice his speeches a hundred times until they seemed spontaneous; I think it important to get down the basic ideas and then rework them, a lesson I learned from my parents

3:11:00 I have never been to Poland and it does not attract me; it seems like a country of sadness and loss; my sister has been and has encouraged me to go; I may do so but it has not drawn me; my mother's father was a famous publisher in Warsaw and their home was a cultural centre for writers, particularly Yiddish writers; Poland was the largest Jewish community in the world at that time; my mother was very much the academic and studied widely; she went to Berlin in 1928 to study; her younger brother Didek - the family name was Szymin - became the world famous photographer David Seymour and used the nickname Chim; that remains an important thread and inspiration in my life as I am responsible for his estate and interest in his work continues to grow; the path of being a photo-journalist was one that I considered; my visual orientation was very much inspired by my knowledge of him; he with Henri Cartier-Bresson and Robert Capa founded Magnum, the photo-cooperative, in 1947, and it continues in London, New York, Paris, Tokyo, as a leading and respected creative community of photographers; on my father's side, they were from more humble origins, from a small town called Kazimierz; my grandfather was a shoemaker of the upper shoe, not the sole; my grandfather married Sara (Mandelbaum), had several children, and then she died; he then married her younger sister, Chana, and had further children; my father was the second youngest of eight children by Chana, so I had many uncles and aunts and cousins; my parents left Warsaw in the early 1930s to join the intellectual movements in Paris, as did my uncle David Seymour and other family members; they travelled and wrote in Spain on the Spanish Civil War; my father wrote a book on it in Yiddish in 1938 (*Krieg in Spanien - War in Spain*) which included ten photos by David Seymour, so there was that collaboration between them; other uncles and cousins came to the US, to Venezuela, France and Spain, as a result of the War; the concentration in New York of family was a very rich source in my growing up; they had a country house in a small place called Lake Peekskill, an hour's drive north of Manhattan; by the time I was four the family had got together and bought a twenty-six acre farm in Flemington, New Jersey, an hour west of Manhattan; the plan was that my oldest first cousin, Paul, and his wife, Judy, who had come out of the Concentration Camps, and were unhappy working in Manhattan in the garment district, should go there; they joined other survivors who had moved to that area; they started an egg farming business where I would go as a child; it was a wonderful opportunity as there were lots of adult figures and cousins; we would work on the farm shoveling manure, collecting eggs, gardening, and was a great experience as a child up to high school years; there were many ways that it formed me positively, with the sense of community and shared experience; I think the parents were drawn together as survivors of the Holocaust and needed each other, and it was not always easy for them, but it was great for us kids; the multiple adult role models were important because my parents had a unique (?) way, working very hard with the demands of their new life; my father had a full time day job doing publicity and his writing was night time work, and there was not a lot of room for other things; my sister recalls that in a less happy way and she wanted more attention; I as a boy was possibly more independent, and had my cousin, George, in the same building; there were nice ways that I could compensate but I certainly saw that my parents were working hard, maybe that was one lesson, and I saw this process of writing and what they were after, their commitment to social causes, social justices, to issues after the Holocaust, important questions that I was inspired by; on the other hand, even from the time of being a teenager I had explicitly set the goal to be not like my father; he was absorbed with his work and his writing and had little time for vacations, hobbies, or anything else; he had little time too for me as a child; I have a few nice memories of him building a sand box for me, walking with me, and taking me to his work at the United Nations where he was a founding member of the UN Correspondents Association, and visits to the Yiddish Press in Manhattan where he worked; I was largely on my own and found my own way, but because of the farm, and early on sharing an apartment with an aunt and uncle, Collette and Chaim (Penchina), and their son Claude who became an important influence on me; he became a physicist and a professor, and was the only academic role model that I had; going through the school system in New York was very good, with the same group of kids from third to sixth grade, and then on through high school; I went to the Bronx High School of Science, a famous school in New York City, one of three where you were admitted by exam.

13:10:22 I went to local public schools - P. S. 75 Emily Dickinson School; we were the first students in that new red brick building which still exists; it was a nice experience; there were wonderful teachers who I still remember, and the constant set of students from third to sixth grade were a special group of about thirty; they all lived within walking distance so I came to know them and their families, and my parents came to know them too; the majority were Jewish as were the teachers; of the teachers I remember, for example, Miss Rosenberg in fifth grade; they were warm, caring types who motivated us to do well; at that time I was a normal boy, taking apart clocks etc., but with cousin Claude as an inspiration I was supposed to be doing science; I did science fairs and built projects while in that school, then in junior high school; in New York there was a special SP (Special Progress) course where you did the seventh to ninth grades in two years, then ten to twelve was high school; there was a competitive atmosphere but a good supportive one; in junior high school I had memorable teachers; Mr Scavone, an Italian, remains a vital figure who pushed us all; he taught social studies but was also our home room teacher; he was into theatre and would study the upcoming Broadway plays; remember Anne Bancroft starring in the Helen Keller story, 'The Miracle Worker', which we went to see soon after it opened; he would take us once or twice a year to plays; I remember the punishment he meted out when one of the students said that they really wanted to go to the play as they would miss regular classes, and he cancelled all the tickets to remind them that devotion to schoolwork was first and that plays were extra; the thirty of us in the special class were sent to another school on the edge of Harlem in a much more difficult neighbourhood, where most of the students were struggling academically; there was an attempt to build up the school and somehow it was hoped that we, bright, motivated kids, would raise the standards; I don't know whether it worked or not; after that I went to the Bronx High School of Science; there were three such schools in New York at that time; one, Stuyvesant, at that time did not take girls, and that decided my choice of Bronx Science even though it was further to travel; it was a wonderful school with inspirational teachers; I remember the physics teacher particularly; I was in that class when someone came in to announce the death of J.F. Kennedy in November 1963, and that is one of my moments frozen in time; by that time I was beginning to concentrate on physics and it was possible to take college level physics in the high school; the advanced placement group of physics students was a wonderful bunch of people; there was one girl in the class whom I took to the high school prom; since we travelled for forty-five minutes on the subway to get to school and back, there was actually little socializing after class, no community of people that were your neighbours as people came from all over the city; then I went to City College of New York

20:17:14 At school we also did plays; I remember playing Nikita Khrushchev in one play and for some reason having to sing 'Yes, we have no bananas'; I also enjoyed P.E. (Physical Education) but I was not especially strong; I liked to play baseball and was pretty good, probably helped by the hours playing on the farm; we would also sometimes play after school near home; when I was in High

School I was selected to be on a city wide science radio programme and my mother would take me possibly twice a month for a one hour discussion by students on science topics; I began to develop my voice; I continued doing science projects - building a solar furnace with a Fresnel lens, a thermo-electric pile to generate electricity from heat, and projects of that sort; the construction mechanisms of building and making such devices, also telling the story on posters we would create; somewhere I have various medals given as prizes at these science fairs; science was an attraction, but so was speaking and being on radio; I had seen my father giving public lectures and also talking on radio and TV, so I had his role model and inspiration so it was not a trouble for me and I was effective at doing it; giving a lecture is a form of performance, of theatre, and one has the responsibility to make the work interesting for my classes and students; I do between forty and fifty public lectures a year; I have always been close to music but it wasn't quite my thing; my sister was a pianist and would perform as a college student; my mother would take me to performances of classical music; at one time I was given piano lessons but didn't take to it; I wish I had more skill in performing, although I enjoy singing it is not something an audience would enjoy; I listen to a wide range of music, both classical and folk; I don't work with music in the background nor go jogging with music in my ears

26:26:17 My father had more of a religious training at a traditional Heder, and he was quite knowledgeable and skilled at reading from the Torah in Hebrew; I went to a Hebrew school after regular school and had Bar Mitzvah at thirteen, and was quite absorbed by it; it fitted in with the sense of community in Upper Manhattan at that time; my father's work in Yiddish was also related to Jewish communities; but it was more secular and we never were a Kosher household though we participated in the holidays; I am a member of a rather unorthodox Jewish group in Washington that functions best as a community whose main form of ritual was the pot-luck dinner; that seems a positive thing; I am very proud of my Jewish heritage and background, which I find interesting and I stay connected to it, but it does not take the form of religious practice and I have drawn further away from the God emphasis; I see it as a cultural and community identification; on the question of whether I am an atheist or not, I try to evade it, not even thinking it important enough to worry about; I don't believe in God or an afterlife; I am sympathetic to Richard Dawkins' 'God Delusion', but I don't want to spend the time reading the book; there are important issues in the world; the Jewish notion of tikkun olam which means to mend the world, is one that I attach to most strongly; the sense that the world we have come to is flawed and each one of us has to do their part in mending it; I take that as an important value, and notions of social justice, equality etc. all influence my science and practice as well as the things I choose to work on; that seems the important obligation that each of us has; I try to inspire my students and others in a practical way to take up these causes, to make the world a better place

30:48:03 Although, as a Jew, there is sometimes the feeling of being an outsider, but it is not a dominant issue; I feel very self-confident and clear in my direction; I have a hard time making the choices of what I should and should not do; the group I belong to in Washington has holiday celebrations which I enjoy going to when I can, but it is okay to miss it; it is a very accepting group that feels there is room for diversity, and for people who are not Jewish to participate, intermarry, and so on; I am familiar with the issue but don't find it a troubling one; I am satisfied with my choices in life and what I have accomplished, though of course there are unfulfilled agendas

33:27:02 I followed an understandable and familiar New York trajectory through Bronx Science (High School) to City College; I arrived there in 1964 and spent four years there; it was quite wonderful; it is a well-established institution and it is free; now there is a modest charge, but all my education was free; it was a wonderful intellectual community; at the time there was a lengthy article in the New York Times describing it as the proletarian Harvard which fitted very well; earlier on it was a hotbed of the immigrants of the 1930s and 40s who were more socialist oriented; by the time I arrived it was much more just a strong intellectual source; it had some distinction of more Nobel prize-winners - Salk, for instance, came from there; Blacks, Jews and other minority groups could get an exceptional education, and was distinguished by admission by examination; when I graduated in 1968 they changed the policy to be by open admission and it essentially destroyed the institution; recently they have restored its exclusivity and hence its reputation; it is a troubling issue because we would like to be broad and welcoming to everyone, but there is a great satisfaction of that distinctive community which sought excellence, dealing with students who could not afford the opportunity; choosing college is maybe an interesting point; I see such a difference now with my students or my own children; they talk about all the colleges, they travel and visit them; at the time I was graduating from High School I had no one to guide me and had little choice as I was interested in physics, City College had a strong reputation in physics, so I went there; I didn't visit any other colleges, neither did my parents know much or invest much effort on my behalf; my sister had gone to Brooklyn College, another branch of City University, so it was just the natural thing to do; it was a good experience; I began to exercise my visual side with photography and for three years I was the photo editor for the Year Book and carried my camera every day and photographed sports events, lectures etc.; I built enough of a portfolio to have an exhibit of some forty to fifty photos by the time I graduated; my uncle had sadly been killed in 1956 in Suez while photographing for Newsweek; that was another memorable and tragic moment; my mother heard of the death of her brother on the news and that day still remains in my mind, I was nine years old; the incident was four days after the armistice; the story continues to unfold as just this month we received information about a detailed report on his death which we had not known of before; there are various controversies of whether it was Egyptian fire or British fire; the jeep that he was riding in, driven by Jean Roy of Paris Match who was a kind of wild adventurer, my uncle much more careful type, just drove through the lines and didn't observe the order to stop, and the Egyptian gunner shot their jeep up and it fell into the canal; it remains a story of vivid memories that keeps unfolding; there will be two upcoming exhibits about his work and I spend ten to fifteen percent of my time on his estate; yesterday I was at the V&A where I have donated some vintage prints to their collection; I also work with other museums like the International Center for Photography in New York, the National Gallery of Art in Washington, George Eastman House in Rochester etc., to promote and preserve his work; it is an interesting other side and I like to have multiple

aspects to my life and work; this brings me into contact with a
completely different set of people

39:19:24 So I was in City College and had a fruitful time, also
pushing forward on the physics agenda where I was not doing well;
that was a surprise and a challenge; I was supposed to be a smart
kid, but I was not enjoying my physics, despite having wonderful
teachers; I was doing fine in mathematics and other subjects, but
once physics left the physical reality of pendulums and rolling balls
and went to more abstract worlds of quantum and electro-
dynamics, the abstractions got further away from me; I was working
for my junior summer for a group of physicists and that was where
I came into computer programming; I was working for this very big
group, Bachman, Baumel and Lea, three City College physicists
with Brookhaven Laboratories connections, aged eighteen; I was
responsible for the computing side, data analysis of these bubble
chamber photographs; we got a day at the Brookhaven eighty inch
bubble chamber; you take 300,000 photographs and then you have
three-dimensional views, and digitise the tracks, and then
reconstruct in three dimensions what the path of the particle was,
knowing what the magnetic field is, seeing the curvature, you know
what has happened with the collisions; I started in the summer,
sometime in June, and I was to take over the programming work of
another student who had graduated; I had a very hard time getting
into it, and learned a lot, and still in my mind is 8/8/66 was the day
I finally succeeded in getting the program to work; the magnetic
tape reels remained on my desk for two years, reminding me of the
day I could begin to call myself a programmer; it was at that time
that I met my dear buddy Charles Kreitzberg who was a young
programmer working for the Computer Center and he helped me
get things done; in the basement of Shephard Hall I had an office,
and felt quite the man about campus as a junior and a senior, and
at a certain point I became the supervisor of our computer; we got
one of the early PDP8 computers, a refrigerator-sized box, and that
was where I began to work, processing our own data in addition to
the larger IBM mainframe; going to classes began to interfere with
my learning; I had become absorbed with learning how to do all
this stuff, and it was a great passion and intensity for those few years
to make these programs work; there was a contrast between the
physics I studied which became increasingly abstract, and the work

of the physicists which I saw with Bachman, Baumel and Lea, where we had published a paper on the Y star 1616 resonance based on the data we had accumulated; I am acknowledged at the end; although I worked for very many hours on it I came to understand that the physicists had initiated the work and that I was merely carrying it out; that kind of abstract discovery of the Y star 1616 resonance was then challenged by others who said there was a mistake in our analysis; that abstract world of physics, the time frame of taking the photographs, two years processing, publishing a paper and getting challenged over a long period, was a dramatic contrast to the immediacy of submitting a deck of Fortran programs and it either ran or it didn't; if it didn't run it was my fault and if I fixed it and it did run, it was my success; there was a great sense of mastery and the cause and effect of my activity; I clearly had a capacity with this important skill using Fortran and other kinds of programming so I got quite strongly into this; I was also influenced by a teacher, Richard Hamming, a key figure in the history of computing; he was working in Bell Laboratories across the river in New Jersey and he came to City College to teach; I had two semester courses from him which I remember vividly because he filled the two semesters only with material that he had invented; he was very much in early numerical analysis programming; his book had the quote: "The purpose of computing is insight not numbers"; that has remained and I have used that phrase, and I say the purpose of visualization is insight and not pictures, so I have played on that; Hamming was certainly an inspirational figure who by his leadership in the field and his strong sense of his own contributions, provided a pretty potent example; this was before there were computer science departments or courses anywhere, and so we had a special opportunity to have him as our instructor

46:58:05 I use the word insight to mean a substantial jump in understanding which has some significance in the world; a former student of mine, Chris North, has taken that and tried to make insights his thing, and has measured the number and kinds of insights that people get using visualization tools; so it has become a notion that people find important because visualization and insight are natural partners, you see something, you understand something you didn't understand before; it might have cause and effect relationships, it might be anomalies, outliers, clusters, patterns, gaps, relationships - these are the kinds of features I would say are the components of an insight; I would say the insight needs to be more than the abstract, statistical or visual detection of an anomaly; it has to be related to the application domain and the significance of the insight; a mere insight that notices that one point is away from a cluster is not significant, but why it is there and how one might use that is important; I would say overall my perception of science and of my work is about cause and effect, and about the capacity to take insights and put them to work for future decisions; an insight is a momentary point, and there might be several of them which might lead you to a larger paradigm shift; insights are not mysterious to me, they are sometime 'ah ha' moments that I certainly have and experience with wonder and glee, but I see that the pursuit of insights is a much more systematic and methodical process; that we can organize ourselves so as to make insights, and that most of what I do, whether discoveries or innovations, are by a systematic way of proceeding and then recognising when there is something important about an insight; Poincaré moments are ones of preparation, incubation, illumination, verification; I very much invest myself in a problem, you become immersed in it and look at it in many different ways using the large set of skills developed to look, potentially understand some relationship or anomaly, and at some point you may have an 'ah ha' experience; the one that is very clear and I have written about was working on the idea of what have come to be known as tree maps; I was looking at a way to create a visual representation of the contents of your hard drive; at the time in the Lab we were running we had a Macintosh with a large hard drive of 80mb shared by fourteen users; when that filled up it was a chore to look at all the fourteen users to see how much each person was using and who should I bother about cleaning up their storage space; I wanted to have a single visual presentation that showed me the proportional use; in that case you might think of fourteen rectangles on the screen proportional to the number of bytes being used, but I was after a richer presentation which would be a recursive, with the notional fourteen rectangles broken up into the folders, and folders within folders etc; I had tried many ways of trying to carve up the screen, space filling so that it would fill the screen with no space between these rectangles; I had been working on this for months and drawn many versions but none had really worked; then there I was in the faculty coffee lounge, I wasn't thinking about it, but suddenly had this 'ah ha' moment and saw how to do it; it took me three days to convince myself it was really correct; there was only six lines of code to get this recursive algorithm but there it was; it was very much like Poincaré's description of how he stepped on the stair of the carriage and had the flash about differential equations; I have had a modest number of others, a few problems that I have solved in relaxed moments, but mostly my discoveries come by a much more conscious, systematic approach, working on the problem; I am quite flexible in the way I work; I don't carry a notebook with me; I am a list-maker and very persistent on things; my favourite way is socially working through; I work with my graduate students and we will meet for a few hours once a week and continue to work on a problem that we are dealing with; for example, we are now working on electronic health records; I have 10,000,000 patients and I think of each patient as having a series of events of different types; what I am interested in finding out is whether there are patterns in these event streams of these patients that have not been noticed before; can you specify a search that will give me all the patients that have more or less of a certain pattern, and what do I mean by more or less; this is a new problem called nearest neighbour problem in K dimensional space; it has an unique problem in that if we had a case in which all the patients had the same events in the same order and we only had to deal with the differences in the timing between them, that is easy; but we have a nastier problem because sometimes we have missing events, sometimes the orders are changed, and there is an additional event, so you get these nasty metrics for nearest neighbour which deal with two measures, one of how similar in time and also we have exact numbers of events, or are there switches, insertions, or deletions; there are different ways to solve the problem so they are implementing software and I am thinking about it, and in these weekly discussions they will propose something and I will agree or suggest something else; I am also very strong and broad in reading of background literature; I say to my students, even undergraduates, that I expect them to read every paper that has ever been written on the problem they are working on; they are quite stunned by that idea, but that forces them to choose something narrow enough that they can accomplish that; again I see it as a social thing and suggest they write to the authors of the papers and send them their draft; they are quite stunned by that, but many times they are graduate students like themselves, or young professors; even senior professors will be responsive if you approach them with specific questions about their work and show an interest in them; I am very much devoted to the idea that you should be willing to send your draft paper to all the people you reference; I have a very wide net of people I approach; I make my work much more social than my colleagues do; most computer scientists have a more introverted approach; I feel I should be willing to let them challenge my work even at an early stage; if I am afraid to show it then there is something wrong; it is fun tracking down literature on the area that I am working on; tracing back to my family background which was very much in the humanities; my sister became a professor of English, my parents were journalists with literary and political interests, so part of a very different world from that of science; I kept their world as very much a part of my life, so my struggle with physics at college was partly because I was so interested in other things; I was very influenced by Marshall McLuhan whose writings had a great impact on me; I went to see him and heard his lectures in New York; he was like his writing, a wild character; he was Professor of English at University of Toronto and had these fantastical ideas and brought together stuff, created a language of hot and cold media which was unfathomable to most; sometimes just a little weird and contradictory, sometimes brilliant; his point about the global village destroying linearity and sequentiality and privacy, was hard to see but he was right in a metaphoric and a real way; I came to accept that the specialist approach, either you are a photographer or a physicist, you have to major in something, that was really not the way I saw the world; I wanted to do it all and to have these different parts of my life all supported, and McLuhan confirmed that that was Okay, and that a sequence of specializations was a possible compromise, and that has been more the metaphor about how I see my work; on each part I focussed narrowly and in depth, produced an important result, and then consciously I would move on; I did not want to professionally stay in the area of my previous success, but wanted to be the eternal graduate student reading a new set of papers and a new literature that I didn't know before, and trying to understand it, and pick up what I would consider to be the low-hanging fruit in this new area and moving on.

Second Part

0:09:07 McLuhan's notion was very important to me; as a student I printed up little business cards saying 'Ben Shneiderman general eclectic - Progress is not our most important product' which was a play on the General Electric slogan of the time; I came to accept the idea that I may not be the best at any specialism but I might be the best generalist; though in that competitive atmosphere that I was in to succeed you had to be the best of something, a harder thing to do was to be the best generalist; professionally it is not an ideal choice although it has been useful and satisfying in my life; those who chose a specialist path and follow it have an easier career; my own approach meant I had to go from interest to interest, whether photography or physics, computing and applications of computing into many different fields; I have collaborated with political scientists, English scholars, chemists, and biologists, and I find these enriching, and have given me a set of multiple perspectives that I find useful for almost any problem; I can make conversation in a lot of different circumstances; I came to feel that after six months of working on a problem with political scientists about Supreme Court and District Court citations over a hundred and fifty years, I was knowledgeable enough to make contributions in the field; the political scientists would publish their findings while I would publish the computer aspects with my students; so the capacity to look at a problem both as a specialist in one problem but generalizing to another problem is probably my best skill; five or six years ago I began to work with molecular biologists about gene expression data analysis; I found it fascinating but a bigger mountain to climb than anything I had done before; after three and a half years of working on it, producing results, I did not feel I had achieved that proficiency to be able to discuss and carry forward in that field; I had a weaker high school biology training and the gap between what I knew and what I needed to know was quite large; I had thought our work should get an acknowledgement but the ethic in biology is that all names go on papers, so there are papers that I am author of but I could not explain them to you adequately; it is a challenge to me, because the conflict between disciplines and their ways of working is unsettling; I felt for a while that I should put those biology papers in a separate section of my resume because I didn't feel I could claim the content of those articles; it is certainly different from computing where individual authors or small groups would be typical; however, the eclectic style of working suited me and I enjoyed the sequential relationships with professionals in different fields to solve their problems and stimulate our work in terms of new problems; the current example of electronic health records is yet that problem again; I think working in medical computing is a noble application of computing which is in harmony with this tikkun olam notion of mending the world; we also broaden computer science not only by its application but by bringing new problems that had not been attended to before; my colleagues think that when I work with English professors that I am doing them a favour; they rather disparage true interdisciplinary work but these English scholars are brilliant and the challenges they bring to us are a novel and important expansions of computer science; by having this sequence of collaborations and working in interdisciplinary teams I do have to establish the ground rules with the scholars that we are not there as their programmers, but are partners; we need to publish in the computing literature and my students need to get PhDs in computer science not merely programming for them; this they come to understand; we have been successful as a group as we have kept explicit several of those principles; the breadth of my reading is great, not just in computer science, but in the broader areas that I have worked in

9:04:04 On graduation from City College with a bachelor's degree in maths and physics I was looking to go to graduate school in computer science; by that time I was more knowledgeable about which universities were good or bad; the favourite place was Carnegie Mellon University to work with Allen Newell and Herb Simon who were then working on the early stages of artificial intelligence; I went to Pittsburgh, paid my down payment, excited that there was a teletype in the basement of Mudge Hall near my dormitory; the Head of Department was Alan Perlis, a famous computer scientist; the thrill of going to work for Newell was very much on my mind, but it was the time of the Vietnam War and the US draft board had said that my going to graduate school was not an acceptable deferred occupation; Carnegie had given me a fellowship and they then gave me an instructorship so that I would be working; I returned to my local draft board and they still said it was unacceptable; this was problematic and I wound up going to teach at a two-year college on Long Island; I was invited to be a full-time instructor there in the Department of Data Processing; Harold Highland was the department Chair and he took a liking to me; he had a son my age who was in similar circumstances so understood he was helping me; my draft board took this to be my national service; I taught fifteen hours of classes a week on Fortran and data processing equipment in a vocational environment; you teach people a very professional skill and they get a job doing that; I taught there for three years; I worked hard and that is how I came to be at the State University of New York at Stony Brook, also on Long Island near Brookhaven Labs; it was a new university and I came to take classes there; computer science was now emerging as a discipline, there was a department but as yet, no degree; I was also doing applied mathematics; I became the first PhD in computer science at Stony Brook in 1973; another colleague of mine there, John Hennessy, is now the President of Stanford University; we had a good group there among whom was Isaac Nassi; the university, being new, was not a very supportive place; my memorable moment outside my office - (I had come as a graduate student but had become an instructor) - there was an open steam vent which they were working on, and one night a student fell into it and died; it was that kind of lack of care which typified the place; however I had a couple of excellent instructors, Herbert Gelernter among them, an early pioneer in artificial intelligence, geometry theorem proving; his classes were magnificent; remember a conflict I had with him when I had got excited about doing some of the theorems; I offered to write a theorem proving program, which was pretty ambitious, if he would excuse me from the mid-term exam; he refused and really annoyed me, though I think he may have been right to force me to do the basics; my own professor there was Jack Heller who had worked on databases and mathematical theory of same; it was there also that I learnt the practical connection because he had been working on museum databases, and we worked on the Museum of Modern Art's fine arts catalogue; my dissertation was a theory of these richer data structures called 'The Graph Theoretic Model of Data Structures' (editor: correct title is Data Structures: Description, Manipulation and Evaluation); it had the application from the Museum and also the generalization of the mathematical theory of graphs; I was able to apply graph theoretic strategies to making efficient models of how to implement these things; I had begun the dissertation writing process in the way that I now work with my students; the traditional approach would be to do your work, then write your dissertation, and then publish your papers from that; I was much more into doing the work, publishing four papers, then writing it as an integrated document to make the dissertation; the advantages there was in harmony with my social approach, to get your work out and let people read it, criticize you and find out what is wrong with it in time for you to make changes and adjustment to it; it also pushed me towards having the work done so it could have an impact on the Museum of Modern Art, and other museum projects that Heller was working on; the other point is that real work should be applied; I don't subscribe to the strong separation between basic research and applied research; I think you do your best basic research if you have a real problem; I follow this with my students, even undergraduates, that you must have somebody outside the classroom for whom you are building this; that has been a very productive approach for all students; I see so many times papers that are done in an abstract way; it is true that maybe twenty years from now somebody will find an application, but I don't have time to waste on abstract problems

18:53:24 I met Ted Codd - very British - I was a very early player in that space of relational data model; he was a wonderful inspiration; his February 1970 paper certainly was one of those important moments where he not only presented an idea but also its ramifications; I was at that time working on those problems and visited him at IBM; one of the papers written for my PhD was published in 1973 called 'Optimal Database Reorganization Points'; one of the issues at that time was when you added or deleted items from a database it would become less efficient, and each successive query would take longer; the desire is to reorganize often but that is costly, so you need an optimum strategy; I had a very lovely solution for that, a fairly mathematical piece, which stimulated thirty-five papers in the next few years on this topic, and opened up a new field; as a graduate student that is the kind of thing you want to see happen and that was one of the components of the dissertation; as a graduate student I had been a volunteer for the ACM at a professional event, and hosted the British software engineer, Michael Jackson; he came to speak in New York and was proposing these new notions of structured programming; rather than the 'go to' of Fortran it had a set of structures of 'if then else, do'; Jackson presented this idea and it seemed a natural jump; if you don't have 'go to' then the flow charts that were popular with arrows connecting to boxes were also not valuable; you had instead recursive structures of 'if then else', then looping structures and sequential execution; there was a nice mathematical proof that those three structures provided all the power that you needed in programming; I began to draw boxes nested within boxes and developed a set of box shapes that would represent this; it was a fifteen minute invention while listening to his talk; I returned to Stony Brook and showed my colleague Isaac Nassi as he was working directly on that for his dissertation; he got excited as he knew the justifications and why, and together we wrote this up and he helped expand the idea; we called them structured flow charts - known as Nassi-Shneiderman diagrams, NSD - Nassi prevailed on me to make an alphabetical order to authorship; we submitted this for publication in the 'Communications of the ACM' and it was returned in a few weeks rejected; the rejection letter said the authors should collect all copies of the paper and burn them; quite a shock for a graduate student to get something like this, made me think I might be on to something; others thought it was clever, innovative, useful, so I had sent it to a few people; one was a senior colleague whom I respected; he didn't respond, but a few months later another colleague sent me tear sheets from a popular science magazine in which he had published this idea under his name; that was really troubling as a graduate student; people said I should file a complaint to the professional society; I just left it and for many years it troubled me as many of the books mentioned his name; eventually this got sorted out and it's widely known as Nassi-Shneiderman diagrams; we then published this article in a non-refereed newsletter of one of the professional societies for programming languages and there are thousands of citations to this paper, hundreds of software packages, patents that follow this, there is an international standard for doing these things; again it was one of those wonderful fifteen minute innovations that we did very little to promote but travelled very well; it is less used now as are most of these diagramming techniques, though it is still widely used in Germany; it is a great episode about the paths of creativity and how certain ideas travel well; maybe the first hundred papers were variations on the theme; it was a simple idea that people could understand and opened up the door to many possibilities; I finished my degree in 1973 and took a position at Indiana University as Assistant Professor; I had recently married and went off to do my service to the mid-west of the US; at that point I was quite strongly motivated to repay my debt to the state universities where I had studied, and Indiana University was a state university; it is a small university town at Bloomington with a small campus; there were five of us junior professors hired the same year, all with families and all Jewish; we became close and all had children; it was a nice experience for three years, and my daughter, Sara, was born in Indiana in 1975; after that, the desire to get back to the East Coast and its neuroses was attractive; I would have liked to have been closer to New York and to family but my wife wanted to be further away; the compromise was to come to College Park at the University of Maryland; there was a particular attraction there because there was a senior faculty member, Ed Sibley, who was head of a small department called Information Systems Management which dealt with the database issues for which I was making my reputation; Sibley was interested in my work on experimental studies of programmers initially; I had learned my trade as a psychologist at Indiana University which had a first rate psychology department with B.F. Skinner; one of the young faculty members there, Richard Mayer, taught me psychological experimentation and I taught him about computing and together we did some good work; he has gone on to a distinguished career in the University of California, Santa Barbara; that was a good partnership and I was gaining some reputation with early studies about programmers; when I was at City College I described working on Fortran and my friend Charlie Kreitzberg and I wrote a little guidebook on how to do good programming in Fortran; we eventually wrote this up in a book 'The Elements of Fortran Style' in about 1971; it had a moderate success and inspired a whole series of other books, but we certainly started that trend; it was a series of rules about how to write good programs, the choice of variable names, modular design, indentation, commenting, a variety of stylistic issues; those were really conjectures based on our experience; I became imbued with the notion of conducting empirical tests where I would make a good and bad version and give them to someone to debug or interpret and I would measure their performance; I was able to alter the independent variable and measure the dependent variable, and that is the way these experiments began; when I came to Maryland this Information Systems Management Department was in the Behavioral and Social Science School not in computing; that was a very interesting opportunity; it was close to the Psychology Department so I was attracted to that; Ed Sibley had been a collaborator and had been helpful to me; early on he had engaged me in doing short courses around the country and abroad on database technologies, before I got my PhD; we had a very good group at Maryland which did well; however it was a small group and eventually lost the political battles; that department was dissolved and most of the faculty left; two of us went to Computer Science so I went to my natural home; I was not especially welcome there as I was seen as a little different; I was into these psychological studies and not especially celebrated; when you bridge into interdisciplinary and newer areas you are going to have some trouble with some fraction of the established community; I had got tenure based on traditional computer science and had demonstrated my mathematical skills

34:37:19 I enjoy lecturing and teaching; early on when it was difficult to get funding for research on the psychological experiments of programmers, I would put my students to work and would make their semester projects to be an empirical study; I was most proud to be able to publish in professional journals with my undergraduates; colleagues disparage that by saying that if the work is so simple that an undergraduate can do it, it can't be very good; but I had done the mathematics, taught mathematical analysis, I can do that stuff, and I moved on to these newer forms which were fun for me; when Sara was in third or fourth grade computing was all the rage at the time; her teacher came and asked me to recommend a textbook to enable them to teach the children the language Basic programming; I was appalled to find that the books were either trivializations or if they taught you programming they depended on high school mathematics; I quickly wrote them about seventy-five pages of programming introduction where the examples were all graphical which kids could understand; it worked well for her class; the DC school system asked me to polish it and they printed 3,000 copies for summer computer camps; we did them for four different computer systems and Sara worked through the problems for one of the versions; I used to help my children with their science projects; I remember one of them was using the sound generator on a computer to generate sound at different pitches and volumes, and to see what was the difference that people could determine, in amplitude or frequency

38:50:18 By 1980 I had taken the different work I had been doing on the experimental studies of programmers and wrote a book called 'Software Psychology', a kind of marriage of disciplines; it was taken up by both computer science book of the month clubs and became a hot topic; by 1982 a group of us were meeting in Washington; I had been the organiser of the Software Psychology Society whose claim to fame was "no members, no officers, no dues"; we had a mailing list of 600 and forty to sixty showed up each month at George Washington University and I organized the speakers; for twenty years this was a very influential group that had both local and national impact; we decided to run a conference in 1982 where we hoped to bring together two to three hundred people; it was held at the National Bureau of Standards and Technology and we drew over 900 people; people were suddenly interested in the topic; the personal computer had appeared though it was still in the days before the Apple Macintosh, but these ideas were beginning to grow; the following year the ACM Special Interest Group on Computer Human Interaction was formed and they took over the conference, and it has continued to be the main source drawing as many as 3,000 every year; that bridge of disciplines was the natural spot for me to be in and I am pleased that it had succeeded; most computer science courses (departments) have one called Human-Computer Interaction; there is still some resistance in computer departments but it is definitely a well-accepted field; by 1986 I published the first edition of 'Designing the User Interface'; in the fourth edition I was joined as co-author with Catherine Plaisant who had been my research collaborator since 1987, and we have just released the fifth edition this Spring; that has been the main textbook in the field and has helped define it; my satisfaction has been to see that go; the early edition of the book focussed on a small group of users like programmers and medical specialists; by the fifth edition we are talking about four billion cell phone users, Wikipedia and

YouTube - the emergence of these platforms of user-generated content is a remarkable transformation for which I am proud of my role; in some areas it is seen as new stuff and not quite science, but this softer science is the way that many things will go; I have written on the history of physics, chemistry, controlled laboratory science of the natural world which will continue; however, I suggest there is a need for a new way of thinking which I call Science 2.0, published in 'Science'; this suggests that the content and the methods need to be changed as well; my eclectic background gave me the capacity to see this perspective; not everyone accepts it but I think the notion is in the right direction; it shifts the methods from control of repeatable laboratory conditions to case studies and interventions in the way that you can do on the Web and have ten thousand data points in two hours which give you remarkable capabilities; shows the trajectory from traditional computer science to these newer bridging sciences of psychological applications and a larger vision about the transformation of science, always with the intention of making the world a better place; as a profession it is a difficult trajectory to do because I'll never be accepted as a leader in medical computing, but I feel I have made my contribution; by going from one discipline to another you start out again as a graduate student which I am happy to do; McLuhan taught me to be a dilettante and of being an amateur as a virtue, and starting on something new is satisfying as part of my everyday work; another contribution that I am proud of is hypertext; we worked on this in the mid eighties and our contribution was the link; when you click on highlighted words and go somewhere, that was our work; many people had commented on the link which is usually traced to Vannevar Bush's article in 1945 which talked about Memex; his notion of the link was that you type in a code number for a document and your microfilm devise with spin to get you there; we began to develop these electronic encyclopaedias and there was an 'ah ha' moment when we had a videodisc player for the images and a plain green screen for the text; we had captions and descriptions and then a numbered list of where you wanted to go next; in one screen there was a very short caption but a numbered list of Polish poets; the text in the caption and the list of names was almost identical and I asked Dan Ostroff, the programmer at the time, how we could replace the caption but then highlight the names and click on them; that was done and we did a number of studies comparing different forms of highlighting; we developed light blue underscored, Tim Berners-Lee saw that and in his 1989 manifesto for the Web he cited our work; it was a small contribution but had a broad impact and gave us great satisfaction; there is controversy about whether we can take pride in this claim - others were certainly working on this - but we made this particular way of doing it, provided an authoring tool and a rich environment to support all that, and that became the inspiration for Tim Berners-Lee; we had published this under the term 'embedded menus'; Tim was clever enough to call them hot links

49:51:22 Tim Berners-Lee deserves credit for inventing the Web; we were working on hypertext things that ran on a single computer and his mind-blowing idea that you could have such a link and it would jump to another computer across a network to retrieve it was wonderful; I met him before that at the Paris hypertext conference; we were building systems called Hyperties which had a commercial version as well, so we were an active player; we built the world's first hypertext scientific journal - the July '87 issue of the CACM; we did the worlds first electronic book called 'Hypertext Hands On' which was in a paper form but it was the disc that mattered; it is the first book in the Library of Congress that has electronic media as part of it; we definitely made those things happen at scale and in marketable ways to reach thousands of people, including Tim Berners-Lee; I am on his scientific council for the web science research initiatives so see him a couple of times a year

51:17:14 On the future, I have already hinted at some of this in the 2.0 argument but the expansion of social media, of user generated content, the empowerment of individuals, and the restructuring of social and political norms are beginning to happen; as you take Facebook and YouTube and apply them to national priorities like energy, health, education, sustainability, environmental protection, you get a transformative effect; I think that is what is really dramatic; between the fourth and fifth edition of 'Designing User Interface', this has just flourished in a way I would never have predicted; YouTube which wasn't around five years ago is now number three on the Web after Yahoo and Google is a startling indicator; I think those things are only just beginning to unwrap in their implications to society; the new forms of media with the dissolution of newspapers in the US and the profound restructuring of societal norms is yet to be fully appreciated; when journalists ask me what is the next killer app I have a straight answer which is trust, empathy, responsibility and privacy; it is those who understand how to generate trust, support empathy, how to make responsibility for failure and success more clear, and protect privacy, also how to raise the level of motivation so that more people participate and contribute, what's the role of egoism, altruism, communalism, and how do we make these social structures in new ways; that is more or less the way I see the world; revising social structures, political structures, economic structures is a fascinating potent transformation; how medical care with change and people become more responsible for their own medical records and treatment; working on innovative social structures is as interesting to me as working on innovative algorithms or devices; I have had the satisfaction of seeing our more recent work on visualization become a commercial success with Spotfire; the idea which we published in a 1994 paper is still one of the most widely cited in the field with Christopher Ahlberg as a visiting student; he formed the company in 1997 which grew to two hundred people and was bought in 2007; it is nice to see a success story like that, and I think people appreciate our Lab, not only for lots of papers and good students, but we have had success stories on the commercial side too; Spotfire and Treemaps have a dozen or more widely used open source versions as well as others; the intellectual challenge is to know which idea will travel well; I am always trying new ones, putting out seeds, and some go well and others struggle; my efforts working on creativity support tools has produced a moderate result but has not become a large field; other ideas like the link on the Web or the notion of human-computer interaction, some are small focussed, others broader restructuring of disciplines; people think I do good demos, but finding ideas and developing them in a way that has an impact and then communicating them effectively is what our job is; sometimes it works well and sometimes I struggle, but still want to get ideas out there

Other possible volumes

Sciences

Biology, zoology and ethology: Patrick Bateson, Gabriel Horn, Robert Hinde, Michael Bate, Alison Richard, John Gurdon, Horace Barlow, Ken Edwards, Barry Keverne, Vittorio Luzzati, Azim Surani [2 volumes]

Physiology and medicine: Andrew Huxley, Richard Keynes, Yung Wai (Charlie) Loke

Chemistry and biochemistry: Sydney Brenner, Dan Brown, Hal Dixon, Aaron Klug, Frederick Sanger, John Sulston, John Meurig Thomas, John Walker, David King [2 volumes]

Astronomy and cosmology: Antony Hewish, Martin Rees, Neil Turok, Owen Gingrich, Edwin Salpeter

Physics and mathematics: Richard Friend, Dan McKenzie, Brian Pippard, John Polkinghorne, Herbert Huppert, Julian Hunt, Professor John Coates, Sir Peter Swinnerton-Dyer, Jeremy Sanders, Haroon Ahmed, John Simpson [2 volumes]

Computing and technology: Andy Hopper, Ken Moody, Jean Bacon, Hermann Hauser, Keith van Rijsbergen, Ben Shneiderman, Maurice Wilkes

Arts and humanities

Anthropology: currently there are 84 people whose interviews and/or lectures are up on the web. [probably about 10 volumes]

History: 19 historians on the web [probably about 4 volumes]

Sociology: Michael Banton, John Barnes, Andre Beteille, Ronald Dore, Ronald Frankenberg, Stuart Hall, Geoffrey Hawthorn, Michael Mann, David McLellan, Garry Runciman, Richard Sennett, M.N. Srinivas, Peter Worsley. [2 volumes]

Economists: Partha Dasgupta, Wynne Godley, Geoff Harcourt, James Mirrlees, Robert Rowthorn, Richard Smethurst

Literature: Peter Avery, Gillian Beer, Frank Kermode, Christopher Ricks, George Steiner, Toshi Takamiya

Explorers: Ursula Graham Bower, Owen Lattimore, David Snellgrove, John Cross

Musicians and artists: Stephen Cleobury, John Rutter, Antony Gormley, David Willcocks

Demographers: Luigi Cavalli-Sforza, Akira Hayami, James Lee, Osamu Saito, Richard Smith, Tony Wrigley

Theologians and philosophers: Don Cupitt, Simon Blackburn

Law and politics: Tom Bingham, John Machin, Nicholas Phillips, Rosemary Polack, William Waldegrave, Richard Wilson

Ethnographic film-makers: Karl Heider, Paul Hockings, Gary Kildea, Liang Bibo, David Macdougall

Others: Charles Chadwycke-Healey (publisher), Martin Jacques (journalist), Laurence Picken (ethno-musicologist), Colin Renfrew (archaeologist), Don Cupitt (theologian), Simon Blackburn (philosopher), Allan Brigham (road sweeper and Cambridge guide)

Teachers: Andrew Morgan (school – history), David Alban, (school - English), James Campbell (undergraduate – history), Keith Thomas (postgraduate – history), Christoph von Furer-Haimendorf (postgraduate – anthropology)

Acknowledgements and royalties

We would like to thank all those whose interviews are included here for their kind involvement in this project. Many different individuals and foundations, in particular the University of Cambridge and King's College, Cambridge, have supported this work over the years.

A percentage of any royalties will be donated to the Wikipedia Foundation in thanks for the use of materials on Wikipedia. The rest of the profits will be given for the support of further research within the University.

www.ingramcontent.com/pod-product-compliance
Lightning Source LLC
Chambersburg PA
CBHW080556060326

40689CB00021B/4878